The Snader Family Alaskan Cookbook

Snader Family Favorites from the Last Frontier

Over 150 recipes, each with a picture or two of the actual prepared recipe.

By Marlene Snader

Copyright 2016 Matthew and Marlene Snader

All rights reserved.

Graphic design and page layout by Matt Snader

Photography by Matt & Marlene Snader, except for:

Back cover family photo in Nome, Missy Sauder

Page 7, top photo, Missy Sauder

Page 13, bottom photo, Carolyn Rissler

Page 16, 18, 20, 22 children's photos by Missy Sauder

Page 98, Conrad Brubaker family

Page 108, 109 Missy Sauder

Published by Alaska Adventure Books

For information on sales contact sales@AlaskaAdventureBooks.com or call 330-840-2230

ISBN 978-0-692-77752-7

Printed in the United States of America

We have made, and continue to enjoy, every recipe in this book. All food photos were taken by us.

Thanks for taking a look at our cookbook! Inside you find many recipes we enjoy, and some are unique.

Recipe Key:
Tablespoon = Tbsp.
Teaspoon = tsp.
Ounce = oz.
Degree or ° = Degrees Fahrenheit
Inch = "
Pounds = lbs.
Our apologies to our Canadian friends, as everything is in Standard.

Table of Contents

Forward by Matt Snader 6
Marlene's "Side of the Story":
About Marlene Snader 8
Meet the Snader Children 16
My thoughts on "The Limo" 42
How do we stay organized while we travel? 55
How Do I Cope With Alaska? 98
Our Schedules with Chores
 and Homeschooling 101
Gardening in Alaska 106
So What Do I Actually Think of Alaska? ... 108
Our 40 Acres and Cabin 148

Appetizers and Drinks
Cheesy Bacon Dip in a Bread Bowl 24
Queso Dip 25
Crabmeat Bombs 26
Crab Crescents 27
Veggie Pinwheels 28
Buffalo Chicken Dip 29
Blueberry Cheeseball 30
Coconut Crème Pie Dip 31
Fruit Salsa 32
Berry Splash Drink 33
Rhubarb Citrus Punch 34
Lemonade 36
Homemade Sports Drink 37
Orange Chiller Drink 38
Candy Cane White Hot Chocolate 39
Hot Cocoa Gift Jars 40
Pumpkin Spice White Hot Chocolate 41

Breads
Cheddar Bay Biscuits 45
Garlic Parmesan Knots 46
Golden Sweet Cornbread 47
Grits Cornbread 48
Bread Bowl 49
Rolls with Strawberry Honey Butter 50
Strawberry Honey Butter 51
Bannock 52
Fireweed Jelly 54

Breakfast
Enchilada Tortilla Breakfast 57
Raspberry Sweet Rolls 58
Toasted Oats 60
Fruit Parfait 60
Strawberry Cream Cheese Danish 61
Cinnamon Roll Pancakes 62
Peanut Butter Cinnamon Rolls 64
French Fry Casserole 66
Breakfast Haystacks 68
French Toast Rollups 69
Cracker Puff 70

Strawberry Rhubarb Coffee Cake 72
Raspberry Muffins 74
Fabulous Fruit Salad 75

Soups and Salads
Kenai Cabbage Salad 77
Dorito Taco Salad 78
Southwest Salad 79
Best Potato Salad 80
Caesar Salad with Homemade Dressing 81
BBQ Corn Chip Salad 82
Yummy Salad 83
Grape Cloud Salad 84
Fluffy Raspberry Salad 85
Applesauce Jello 86
Strawberry Poppy Seed Salad 88
Candied Walnuts 90
Chinese Chicken Salad 91
Gold Miners Salad 92
BBQ Macaroni Salad 94
French Onion Soup 95
Favorite Italian Wedding Soup 96
Creamy Mushroom and Bacon Soup 99
Creamy Sausage Soup 100
Creamy Gnocchi Soup 102
Creamy White Bean & Ham Tortellini Soup 104
Stuffed Pepper Soup 107

Main Dishes
Mexican Stuffed Pepper 111
Bacon Wrapped Meatloaf 112
Almost Lasagna 114
Grizzly Bear Burgers 116
Mongolian Beef 118
Smoked Brisket 120
Zucchini Boats 121
Krunch Wrap Deluxe 122
Latin Tortillas 123
Potato Haystack Casserole 124
Meatball Sub Casserole 125
Enchilada Tator Tot Casserole 126
Kodiak Casserole 127
Honey BBQ Boneless Chicken 128
Loaded Potato Casserole 130
Campfire Chicken 131
Good Chicken 132
Italian Rice Casserole 133
Hawaiian Chicken Kabobs 134
Crockpot Creamy Italian Chicken 136
Baked Ziti with Parmesan Topping 137
Poor Man's Lobster (Halibut) 138
Brown Sugar Rub 139
Heavenly Halibut 140
Tuna Twirls 141
Rachel Casserole 142

Crab Au Gratin	143
Chicken Bacon Ranch Casserole	144
BLT Pizza	146

Side Dishes

Roasted Parmesan Sweet Potatoes	153
Canadian Poutine	154
Cheesy Potatoes	155
Twice Baked Potatoes	156
Buttery Crusted Baked Potatoes	157
Ultimate Scalloped Potatoes	158
Brown Sugar Red Potatoes	159
Lemon Herb Potatoes	158
Brown Sugar Green Beans	161
Hush Puppies	162
Rainbow Roasted Vegetables	163
Honey Roasted Carrots	164
Loaded Roasted Broccoli	165
Egg Salad Divan	166
Cheesy Corn	167
Best Brussel Sprouts	168
Grandma's Filling	169
Zucchini Corn Pancakes	155
Zucchini Pie	171
Zucchini Fries with Onion Dip	172

Desserts

Cheese Tarts	175
Orange Creamsicle Cookies	176
Banana Cookies	177
Peanut Butter Teddies	178
Bigfoot Cookies	180
Alcan Highway Cookies	182
Peanut Butter Winkies	184
Chocolate Peanut Butter Bites	185
Strawberry and White Chocolate Chip Cookies	186
Polar Bear Paws	187
Chocolate Surprise Cookies	188
Almond Joy Energy Bites	189
Avalanche Bars	190
Apple Snickerdoodle Bars	192
S'mores Cookie Bars	193
Oreo Bars	194
M & M Dream Bars	196
Chocolate Revel Bars	197
Chocolate Peanut Butter Dream Bars	198
Triple Chocolate Cherry Bars	199
Chocolate Chip Skillet Brownie	200
Impossible Pumpkin Cupcakes	201
Orange Creamsicle Cake	202
Pistachio Cake	203
Earthquake Cake	204
No Bake Strawberry Delight	205
Strawberry Shortcake	206
Mint Chip Lush	208
Fried Ice Cream Dessert	210
Pina Colada Fluff	211
Mocha Mud Pie Dessert	212
Toasted Coconut Pudding	214
Pistachio Ice Cream Dessert	215
Vanilla Bean Cheesecake	216
Rainbow Jello	218
Reese's Peanut Butter Truffles	219
Pumpkin Roll Cake	220

Forward
By Matt Snader

Many people, after reading our books, have asked "What is Marlene's side of the story?" This puzzled me at first, but I assumed that it must be because everyone must think Marlene to be the most fortunate wife in the world, going along on all these wonderful adventures with such a darling husband. Slowly I began to realize that perhaps this wasn't what they were thinking! And, after some time, dawned on me I am indeed very fortunate to be married to Marlene, as most women wouldn't be nearly as forgiving as she is. Of course Marlene is very modest when I point this out, and she'll even make jokes that make me nervous.

The truth is, I need to appreciate Marlene even more (and 10,000 women nod vigorously while reading this). She is a marvel at multitasking; consider a typical Sunday morning. I will stumble out of bed, and stagger around half asleep looking for something to eat. Eventually I'll manage to make a pot of coffee, feed the dogs, and find my Sunday shoes. Marlene will shout something about "why don't you change the baby" as she runs past. By the time I have the baby changed, everyone is ready for church. In the meantime, Marlene has put together a casserole for lunch, tastefully matched everyone's outfits, combed 5 girls, and located all their shoes. Occasionally I'll still be at the making coffee stage, while everyone is in the van blowing the horn.

If you have ever looked at our family pictures, and thought "wow, it doesn't look like they all just climbed out of a haystack," then you are witnessing Marlene's handywork. If I was in charge of combing hair, making sure the children's clothes didn't clash, or even that they were washed, you wouldn't be thinking such things.

Marlene is an excellent cook. It was only natural when we started selling books, I thought she should make a cookbook. After all, I figured, you just slap some recipes in a book and crank it out. This was a flawed idea. This cookbook has taken more time to put together than any of our other books, without question.

Another unexpected problem was this: There is a cook in the house, every day, for days, baking the nicest and tastiest dishes possible. You may have noticed our cookbook is not designed to make fat people skinny. I thought it would have been unkind not to sample Marlene's hard work. So...I gained 10 pounds. If I look fatter in the pictures from this year (2016) it is because I am. Of course, this was intentional, as I didn't eat any of the food by accident. But winter is coming, and the huskies are restless. I think I'll be able to burn off these 10 pounds without too much trouble.

I made several of the recipes in the book. Marlene was apparently so proud of my cooking and baking skills, she insisted the recipes and pictures I did be clearly marked.

And some consolation, if you're worried about buying this cookbook and becoming fat from the recipes. Think how tragic it would be if you ate nothing but carrot sticks and celery, and after months of this lost all your body fat, and then got caught in an Arctic blizzard and died of hypothermia. As you lay shivering in a snowbank, you would likely regret all those carrot sticks. With that said, I have noticed (often while visiting a buffet) that some folks apparently carry this paranoia to extreme levels. If you notice your body becoming more insulated than what is practical, I suggest making use of the salad section of this book. But don't blame the cook...

Page 7

About the Author – Marlene Snader

People keep asking what is "my side of the story." Well, first let me discuss my upbringing, and my dad. My dad worked at the same job for over thirty years, a job that he started at when he was sixteen. When we took family trips, they were usually planned out almost a year in advance. My dad's shop was always clean, neat, and very organized. The vehicles were always meticulously maintained, and were always rather boring colors, such as solid brown, solid blue, etc. I don't think spray painting his cars camouflage ever crossed his mind. Growing up, I didn't even know Alaska existed.

Growing up, one thing I loved was our family trips. As I mentioned, these were planned well in advance, and I eagerly anticipated them for months. The trips were so well planned, we often returned home with money left over.

Then I met Matt. Matt and I met through his cousin, Ann. Ann was and is still one of my best friends. You may have heard the saying "opposites attract". Matt asked me out on my 18th birthday, and from there things went North (pun intended—you know how if something goes "south" it is considered bad, which is probably not a coincidence.)

On our first date we went camping. This definitely would not be my first choice for a first date. We went with my sister Carolyn and boyfriend Harlan, my aunt and uncle Tom and Anna, my parents, and my youngest sister Gina. The only thing I remember from the first evening is that Tom tried to get everyone to eat camp fire boiled crayfish (sorry, no recipe for that in this cookbook.) I was extremely nervous (and Matt later admitted he was too) for the hour and half ride to the camp site, as we drove there by ourselves. At the campsite Matt and Harlan slept on the picnic tables. I was rather mortified the next morning to find him sleeping soundly on the picnic table and everyone else was around and about.

When we first started dating I noticed subtle differences between him and my dad. He did his best to appear "normal" by replacing his ratty, beat up old mustang with a much newer, nicer one, soon after we started dating. I thought it was a nice touch when he began renting stretch limousines for our dates. Now these limousines weren't fancy chauffeured ones, but ones he somehow talked a car lot owner into letting him use. I should have taken this as a sign of things to come—after all, my parents didn't have a habit of renting limos.

We got married April 12, 2003 at Lichty's Mennonite Church near Terre Hill, Pennsylvania. After renting a house for a year in Adamstown, we purchased a house in Leola, Pa. Around this time Matt started a business fixing computers. The idea of owning and running a business was completely foreign and frightening to me. This was confirmed when the business went south. Through our mistakes God was gracious, and allowed us to build the classified website business of LancasterPuppies.com. One nice feature of this business was it could be managed with a cell phone, computer and Internet connection. This allows work to be done while travelling, but is also the biggest draw back—you can never actually go on vacation with out causing some conflict.

During the computer business years, we managed a one month mission trip to Thailand. Our job was to help babysit missionary children while they had seminars, and we also smuggled some Gospel literature into China (I don't recall my parents ever doing this either). On the flight we had a layover in Alaska, never imagining that this state held such a huge part of our future. While in the Anchorage airport Matt did make the comment that he wanted to "stay in Alaska."

Flying was a huge stretch for me. I had told Matt that he would "never get me in an airplane." Instead of just getting me on an airplane, he talked me literally into flying halfway around the world. This was a very good, stretching experience for me. I think everyone should experience another culture sometime in their lives. During this time we only had Shane. I can't imagine taking such a trip with seven children.

In 2008, we moved to Snyder County, Pennsylvania. This was a big step in the right direction (northwest)... Oops, that was actually something Matt just said. We do both prefer rural living. Kallia was born less than a month after moving to Snyder County.

Around the spring of 2011, we hauled a load of food to an orphanage in Mexico, with our ancient Ford van that we had purchased for $400. The food was provided by Blessings of Hope Food Ministry. We raised money for the trip by selling squares on our van. The way the fund raiser worked, the side of the van was split into many squares. For a donation, people could "buy" a square on the van, and tell us what color to paint it. The result was a paint job that looked like a patchwork quilt. This was actually our only vehicle at the time, and it was not my favorite vehicle to drive, especially to church!

To the shock of everyone, the trip to Mexico (covering 7,000 miles) and back went almost without incident. We had one flat tire on the van, and two flat tires with the trailer. The transmission fluid line disconnected at a truck stop, but that took Matt five minutes to put back together. None of these problems were a big deal.

Crossing into the Mexican border was a mini fiasco. I was stuck in the van while Matt filled out papers at customs. When they searched the van, the border guards found a pack of our gospel tracts that looked like money. This caused a lot of jabbering in Spanish. What they said, I don't know, but they did return everything. The border crossing took the whole day. We sat for hours. And hours.

One funny coincidence was the real money was put in a plastic wet wipe container. This was an attempt to conceal it. Lana was our baby at the time, and somebody wrote "Lana" on the box with permanent marker. Later we discovered "Lana" is slang in Spanish for money!

Because we borrowed the trailer, we did not have our names on the trailer registration, and we couldn't take it into Mexico. Someone loaned us a Mexican trailer that looked as though it would fall apart any second. None of the lights worked, the axles were bent, and the tires were crooked. Despite these issues, we were able to pray the trailer through the last 250 miles of the trip. We were glad for the trailer, but even more glad to arrive at our destination with it in one piece!

Above: The van we drove to Mexico. We pulled an enclosed trailer, filled with food, from Blessings of Hope food ministry, to an orphanage. Below: The town in Mexico where the orphanage is.

In 2013 we made our first trip with Alaska as the destination. We had a little money, and decided "if we don't go now, we might never get to go" (silly us). Unlike my parents' trips, we only had a week to plan this one. To save money we took a portable propane stove along, and made soup along the way. We could have saved a lot of money if we had just eaten peanut butter and jelly sandwiches. While in Alaska, I made the mistake of saying "I could live here".

After our trip, we, I mean Matt, decided to go shopping for land in Alaska. It was exciting to think about building a cabin in Alaska. I was ok with camping while we built the cabin, and enjoyed planning the meals, as long as I knew we weren't be camping long. I'm not some happy, live off land in tents type. Matt thought the cabin would only take a week to construct, and I was ok with camping outside for a week. Somehow though, the cabin did NOT go up in a week, and things took longer than expected. We have since learned to expect this with things concerning Alaska.

The original cabin design was more of a storage shed. Somehow this design got bigger and bigger, which is good, because at the time I didn't expect to live in it. Originally it was planned to be used as a rental cabin but had I known we would live in it, I would have insisted on better kitchen cabinets and flooring.

We returned later that year to Pennsylvania to have Mary Kate. She was born August 21st, 2014. Seven weeks after Mary Kate was born we headed north again. This was a trip I think we all regretted. It is hard enough to adjust to a new baby without dragging yourself and the family 4,400 miles. Upon returning to Alaska, several challenges emerged.

There was not yet a porch on the cabin, and the children all loved playing in the snow. They would drag all kinds of dirt and snow into the cabin, and throw all their shoes and coats inside the door. Half the time I could not do dishes, because the cabin plumbing kept acting up. It seemed the plumbing could tell when it was a Saturday night, and would quit working. This didn't really matter, because by the time we rode the 4 wheelers out the lane to the van, we were all in covered in mud anyway. On the way to church I would do all the girls hair. Since the ride was an hour and a half, it gave me plenty of time. At least this way, their hair was still in place when we arrived (most of the time).

Sometimes I would lay on the sofa in despair. I must admit this was not a highlight in my life. On top of this, we seemingly had vehicle problems every day. One time I actually threw the phone and burst into tears, at the news of another van break down. The reason this upset me so much is that it delayed a trip to Pennsylvania. Typically I do not show my emotions, nor am I normally dramatic. I think Matt was slightly worried over this time.

We decided to return to Pennsylvania for the holidays, and also visited Florida with my sister Carolyn, her husband Harlan, and the rest of the Rissler family. The cousins made lots of good memories playing together and biking in the warm sun. One evening the guys babysat while Carolyn and I took some of the older children mini golfing.

What a contrast—wintertime in Alaska versus wintertime in Florida!

Living with another family for awhile you realize how each family does things differently. Our children tend to occasionally snack before meals. They learned quickly this was not allowed in the Rissler household!

By early next spring, the bad memories had faded, and I was ready to tackle Alaska again. This time, we returned with a motor home. It was fun packing our clothes, planning our meals to cook along the way. I could even do laundry while driving! Eight people (at the time) create a lot of laundry. It has been said "a woman needs a nest", and the motor home provides a sense of this. It made the trip much more enjoyable.

Our goal was to spend at least six months and several days in Alaska a year to have a legitimate claim of being Alaska residents. There was mostly good memories that summer, but some bad. One bad memory was the day Matt brought 1,500 chicks home from the post office. Of course this was the day we were planning to go visit Seward. My sister, JoAnn, and her husband Paul and their family were there. We decided to just put the chicks in the cabin, as they were still in their boxes. The fact the chicks are curious and will escape tiny boxes eluded us. When we returned from Seward, Matt was probably glad we had company, or things may have went south (like the whole motorhome).

Along with Paul and JoAnn's help, the chicks were put in the coop and the floor cleaned up. Five hundred of the chicks were already sold to the neighbor, so Matt and Paul delivered them the next day.

The summer of 2015 we had a lot of company, including Marv and Andi living at our place for a few weeks. This really made time go fast, and the most shocking company was my parents. They came with my younger sister, Gina, her husband Mike, and their three children. Hopefully the next time they come visit they can spend more than just two days at our place.

That summer we also went on a gold panning trip above Fairbanks. I think Matt and the children enjoyed gold panning in the wilderness a lot more than I did. It was a huge chore to keep the motorhome clean, with everyone tracking mud and dirt in and out. Hauling all the prospecting equipment up and down the ravine to the river also took the fun out of it! And we didn't find any gold.

Yes, it's safe to say married life has proven to be different than my growing up years. In Debi Pearl's book *Created to be a Help Meet*, her Mr. Visionary describes Matt. I'm not proud to say I didn't always make the changes with grace, but thankfully God and Matt are forgiving. Matt often says of me "How could you not like a wife like that!" Matt has certainly helped me broaden my horizons, and that, I think, is a good thing. (Note from Matt: Marlene has also been forgiving!)

Debi Pearl also says a wife of a visionary should "hang on and enjoy the ride" and "to enjoy the ride you need to be a little bit reckless and blind in one eye." I do enjoy being with Matt for the ride, wherever that ride ends up taking us.

Above: My parents (John and Mary Martin) with Kallia, walking on our snow covered lane. Below: My sister, Gina, and myself, with several of our children, on the end of the Homer Spit.

Meet the Snader Children:

Dallas

Mary Kate

Dallas Elijah Snader: AKA Dally

Born March 2, 2016

    We all adore his little smile, and being the youngest, has us all wrapped around his little finger. He likes to cry a lot, but is instantly quiet when picked up by one of his loving siblings. Perhaps he is a little spoiled but I guess is it not easy being #7 in the family. He almost showed up in time to be a leap year baby, but I suppose he wanted a birthday that came every year. Matt is hoping he grows up to be a musher like Dallas Seavy, but we'll let that up to Dallas to decide.

Mary Kate Snader: AKA Cheeser

Born August 24, 2014

Mary Kate was named after her grandmother, Mary Martin. You may have heard of the saying "girls are made of sugar and spice...", we think Mary Kate is more spice than sugar, although she can be very sweet sometimes! Learning to walk at nine and a half months, she is very independent. You don't have to wonder what she is thinking or feeling, because she lets all her feelings show! We love getting her to say "baby Musk Ox". She has a stuffed toy Musk Ox that our babysitter, Missy, bought for her on the way back from Nome. Supposedly this Musk Ox is named "Petey." She loves steak and unsweetened iced tea, which seems to me an unlikely set of tastes for a 2 year old. Mary Kate also enjoys going for walks out the lane (with a parent or older sibling, of course).

Top: Samantha

Right: Lana

Samantha Brooke Snader AKA Mancy

Born October 2, 2012

      Samantha is very laid back. When she was younger she looked very much like Matt, so much so that on several occasions complete strangers commented on this. She is very sensitive and loves playing with dolls and pretending house. Mary Kate and her are always getting into things, and you can hear something is going on by her giggling. Samantha loves to be a pupil when Desiree teaches their pretend school. At a young age she started declaring "when she gets big she is going to shoot moose and bears." I thought Matt put her up to this, but he claims he is innocent. She is a great older sister and loves holding Dallas, although sometimes she falls asleep with him crying on her lap. Samantha loves sitting with Judy Eicher in church (one of our friends in Alaska).

Lana Elizabeth Snader, AKA Laney Beth

Born September 15, 2010

      Lana loves animals, so much so the one Sunday morning before church, while dressed in her church clothes, she sneaked outside and held one of the chickens (true story). Lana is looking forward to first grade this year. Very outgoing, Lana is very talkative, and will talk endlessly if given half the chance. Her favorite hobby is drawing and coloring. She also loves playing outside. Lana loves black olives, and will eat them by the handful. She is typically very happy and cheerful, and will be probably grow up to be an optimist.

Right: Kallia

Bottom: Desiree

Kallia Janae Snader, AKA Heimer

Born August 10, 2008

     Kallia is very vibrant and full of life: She is very much a baby person, and loves to take care of babies, however the babies don't always like her because she tends to move too fast. Her curls match her personality! She lives life with a spark in her eyes, and she also wears her emotions on her sleeves, no guessing if she is happy or sad. Kallia claims she doesn't like schoolwork, but she does do well at it. Kallia says when she grows up she wants to be a nurse that works with babies, so hopefully till then she slows down a little bit. It shouldn't surprise anyone she likes 4 wheeler rides. Kallia's favorite dog is our Alaskan Malamute named "Pancake" (picture on right).

Desiree Erin Snader, AKA Nezzy or Dezzy

Born July 28, 2006

     Desiree was born 15 minutes after Matt's birthday (had we been in Alaska, she would have been born on Matt's birthday). She is my dependable, reliable helper. If I need something done, she is the one that can be depended on. Desiree would rather help take care of older children, like Mary Kate, instead of Dallas. She is the most patient and calm one in the family. As a baby she hardly ever cried. Most of the time she is really soft spoken, with some notable exceptions. She just got done spending a few days at the Keystone Rubies Camp, and absolutely loved it. It's good she did, as we drove over 4,000 miles just to take her to camp. She loves sewing, baking and cooking.

Shane Michael Snader AKA Shaner Taner

Born July 13, 2004

       Shane is our firstborn, and was the first grandchild on the Snader side, and the first boy on the Martin side. Shane has an odd sense of humor (we still are not sure where that came from) and loves knock knock jokes, and practical jokes. He does have a side that is mature for his age, and is also sensitive. Because he has so many sisters, he often gets to do things with his dad, such as hunting, fishing, gold panning, etc. He has a surprising talent for filleting fish, and enjoys it so much he will beg to clean the fish. Often he tells me that he can't wait until he is 16, so he can take me out for breakfast. In Alaska, drivers can get their permit at 14, so now he can do this two years earlier. Shane also loves science and reading. He will read stacks of books between Alaska and Pa.

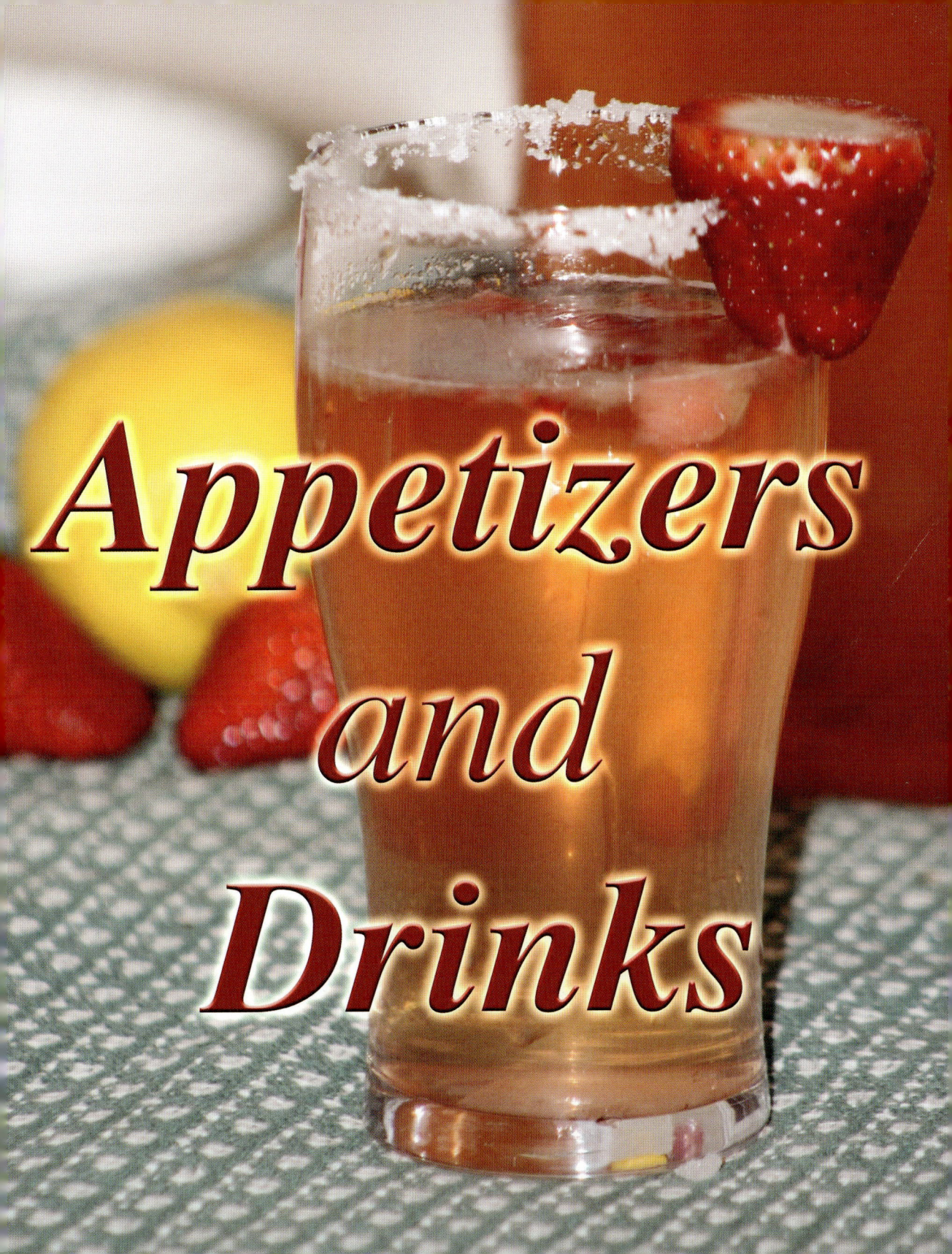

Cheesy Bacon Dip in a Bread Bowl

Ingredients
- 1 round loaf (1 pound) sourdough bread
- 1 package (8 oz.) cream cheese, softened
- 1-1/2 cups (12 oz.) sour cream
- 2 cups (8 oz.) shredded cheddar cheese
- 1-1/2 tsp. Worcestershire sauce
- 3/4 lb. sliced bacon, cooked and crumbled
- 1/2 cup chopped green onions
- Assorted crackers

Alaska was purchased from Russia on March 30, 1867, for $7.2 million. That is about 2 cents an acre!

Directions
1. Cut the top fourth off the loaf of bread; carefully hollow out the bottom, leaving a 1-in. shell. Cut the removed bread and top of loaf into cubes; set aside.
2. In a large bowl, beat cream cheese until fluffy. Add the sour cream, cheddar cheese and Worcestershire sauce until blended; stir in bacon and onions.
3. Spoon into bread shell. Wrap in a piece of heavy-duty foil. Bake at 325° for 1 hour. or until heated through. Serve with crackers and reserved bread cubes. Yield: 4 cups

Queso Dip

Ingredients

- 1 Tbsp. olive oil
- 1 small onion, chopped
- 1 1/2 cups of corn
- 1 red bell pepper, diced
- 2 garlic cloves, minced
- 1 cup salsa
- 1 8 oz. package cream cheese, cubed
- 1/2 cup real mayonnaise
- 1/2 cup sour cream
- 1 tsp. ground cumin
- 1/4 tsp. smoked paprika
- salt and pepper to taste
- 1 cup shredded Monterey Jack cheese, divided
- 1 1/2 cups cheddar cheese, divided
- hot sauce to taste

Directions

1. Heat 1 Tbsp. olive oil in a 12-inch oven proof skillet over medium high heat. Add onions and cook for 3 minutes. Add corn, bell peppers and garlic and sauté for 1 additional minute.
2. Stir in salsa , cream cheese, sour cream, mayonnaise, spices, 3/4 cup Monterey Jack cheese and 1 1/4 cup cheddar cheese. Spread in an even layer and top with remaining cheeses.
3. Bake at 350° for 20- 25 minutes or until bubbly. Broil until cheese is golden.
4. You can transfer dip to slow cooker to keep warm for 2 hours or serve immediately. Garnish with fresh cilantro and chopped tomatoes if desired.
5. Serve with tortilla chips.

Crabmeat Bombs

Ingredients
- 1 lb. crabmeat
- 1 egg, beaten
- 1 cup Ritz Crackers, crushed
- 1 tsp. Yellow Mustard
- 2 Tbsp. Fresh Lemon Juice
- 2 Tbsp. Fresh Parsley, chopped
- 1 tsp. Old Bay Seasoning
- 1 Tbsp. Worcestershire Sauce

Directions
1. Place crabmeat in a mixing bowl, picking any stray shell fragments out. Add crushed crackers, Old Bay Seasoning & parsley to the crab.
2. In a separate bowl, combine egg, mustard, lemon juice and Worcestershire sauce. Whip with a whisk until smooth.
3. Pour egg mixture over the crabmeat and crackers and gently mix being careful not to break up large lumps of crabmeat.
4. Mold into golf ball sized balls and place on a cookie sheet. Bake at 350º for 30 minutes.
5. Drizzle with melted butter and allow to cool.

Crab Crescents

Ingredients

- 1 package Pillsbury Crescent rolls (regular size)
- 6 oz. cream cheese, softened
- 1/2 cup mayonnaise
- 1 1/2 tsp. lemon juice
- 1/2 tsp. Worcestershire sauce
- 1 green onion, finely sliced
- 1/2 can crab meat, drained
- 1 clove garlic
- 1/2 cup and 1/3 cup mozzarella cheese (divided)

Directions

1. Preheat oven to 375º.
2. In a small bowl combine cream cheese, mayonnaise, lemon juice, Worcestershire sauce, green onion, garlic and 1/2 cup mozzarella cheese. Gently fold in crab meat and set aside.
3. Open crescent rolls, pinch seams together and cut into 18 even squares.
4. Place crescent squares in a mini muffin pan and gently press into the cups. Divide filling between wells. Top with remaining 1/3 cup cheese.
5. Bake 12 minutes. Allow to cool 5 minutes before removing from pan.

These are a family favorite!

Veggie Pinwheels

Ingredients
- 8 oz. cream cheese, softened
- 3/4 cup sour cream
- 1 pkg. Ranch dressing mix
- 3 green onions, sliced
- 1/2 of a medium-sized red bell pepper, diced
- 2.25 oz. can sliced ripe olives, drained
- 6 oz. shredded sharp cheddar cheese
- About 7 or 8 flour tortillas
- Extra sour cream to seal the edges

Alaska's population is 52% men, the highest of any state in the U.S. I have heard Alaska called "A man's world." How many woman do you know that can't wait to shoot a moose or grizzly bear?

Directions
1. Soften cream cheese and mix with mixer for a few seconds.
2. Add other ingredients except tortillas.
3. Stir well.
4. Spread a layer of filling on tortillas to the very edge.
5. Wrap each tortilla as tightly as possible.
6. Seal the edges by smoothing a little extra filling or sour cream along the border.
7. Wrap each tortilla in plastic wrap.
8. Place in a zip lock bag and store overnight if possible, but at least four hours so ingredients set.
9. Slice each tortilla into four pieces.

Buffalo Chicken Dip

A great snack for hungry moose hunters coming back from a long day in the woods! Or a good addition to a picnic along a wood stream, while watching the salmon jumping. Also an excellent snack to help stay warm while watching the northern lights on a crisp, cold winter night. If no microwave is handy, a campfire works just as good!

Ingredients

- 1 1/2 cups cooked and shredded chicken or 1 (12 oz.) can chunk chicken, drained
- 1 (8 oz.) package cream cheese, softened
- 1/2 cup Ranch dressing
- 1/2 cup Buffalo wing sauce (such as Frank's Red Hot, not to be confused with their pepper sauce. Start with less if you want and add more to your desired hotness.)
- 3/4 cup shredded Cheddar cheese
- blue cheese crumbles (optional)

Directions

1. Heat chicken and Buffalo sauce in a skillet over medium heat, until heated through. Make sure to break up the chicken so there are no big chunks.
2. Stir in cream cheese and ranch dressing. Cook, stirring until well blended and warm.
3. Mix in shredded cheese.
4. Pour into a shallow dish or pie pan and sprinkle with blue cheese crumbles, microwave it until the cheese melts. We typically only put blue cheese on half of it for those who aren't blue cheese fans. Serve with chips for dipping.

Blueberry Pie Cheeseball

This Blueberry Pie Cheese Ball tastes just like a blueberry cheesecake and is the perfect appetizer or dessert for your next get together! Easy and delicious!

Ingredients
2-8 oz. packages of cream cheese, room temperature
2 sticks unsalted butter, room temperature
1 cup powdered sugar
1/2 cup brown sugar
2 tsp. vanilla extract
1 cup chopped pecans, optional
1 21 oz. can blueberry pie filling
1/2 cup graham cracker crumbs
1/4 cup finely chopped pecans

Directions
1. Cream cheese and butter together.
2. Gradually beat in sugars and vanilla extract.
3. Stir in pecans and blueberry pie filling until completely combined.
4. Line a bowl with plastic wrap and fill with mixture. Make sure the top is covered securely.
5. Refrigerate for at least three hours.
6. Combine the graham cracker crumbs and chopped pecans in a small bowl and set aside.
7. Peel off the plastic wrap on the top and invert onto a serving board or cake stand. Coat the cheeseball with the graham cracker crumb mixture, patting gently to secure.
8. Refrigerate until ready to serve.

Coconut Crème Pie Dip

Ingredients
- 1-15 oz. can cream of coconut
- 1/4 cup milk
- 1 large (5.1 oz.) box instant vanilla pudding mix
- 1-14 oz. can sweetened condensed milk
- 2 cups sweetened flaked coconut, toasted and divided
- 1-8 oz. tub cool whip, thawed
- Graham crackers or shortbread cookies for dipping

Directions
1. Add cream of coconut and milk to a stand mixer or large bowl (using a hand held mixer) and mix on medium speed until smooth.
2. Add pudding mix and sweetened condensed milk and mix until thoroughly combined.
3. Fold in a heaping cup of toasted coconut and cool whip and mix until just combined.
4. Add mixture to a serving bowl and refrigerate for four hours. Garnish with remaining toasted coconut.
5. Serve with graham crackers or shortbread cookies.

Fruit Salsa

Ingredients
- 1 cup finely chopped strawberries
- 1 medium navel orange, peeled and finely chopped
- 3 medium kiwi
- 1 can unsweetened crushed pineapple, drained
- 1 Tbsp. Lemon juice
- 1 1/2 tsp. Sugar

Cinnamon chips
- 10 flour tortillas (8 inches)
- 1/4 cup butter
- 1/3 cup sugar
- 1 tsp. Cinnamon

Directions
1. In a small bowl combine first six ingredients.
2. Cover and refrigerate until serving.
3. For cinnamon chips: brush tortillas with butter.
4. Cut each into eight wedges.
5. Combine sugar and cinnamon, sprinkle over tortillas.
6. Place on ungreased baking sheets.
7. Bake at 350° for 5-10 minutes or until crisp.
8. Serve with fruit salsa.

Berry Splash Drink

A refreshing drink after a hard day of dip netting!

Ingredients
- 1 (0.13 oz.) package unsweetened cherry drink mix
- 6 cups white cranberry juice
- 1/4 cup sugar
- Garnish: fresh mint sprigs or strawberry leaves

Directions
1. Stir together first 3 ingredients and 2 cups water in a large pitcher until sugar is dissolved.
2. Cover and chill. Garnish, if desired.

Note: We tested with Kool-Aid Cherry Unsweetened Soft Drink Mix.

Freeze blueberries in ice for decoration

Rhubarb Citrus Punch

Ingredients
- 8 cups diced fresh or frozen rhubarb
- 5 cups water
- 1-1/3 cups sugar
- 2 cups orange juice
- 3/4 cup lemon juice
- 1 quart ginger ale, chilled
- 1 quart fresh or frozen strawberries, optional
- Ice cubes

Alaska is the westernmost, northernmost, and easternmost state. North and west are obvious, but east not as much. Try not to think about it too much or you may get a headache.

Directions
1. In a large kettle, simmer rhubarb and water until rhubarb is soft. Cool; strain through several layers of cheesecloth. Measure 4 cups juice and return to kettle with the sugar. Heat until sugar is dissolved. Chill.
2. Refrigerate or freeze any remaining rhubarb juice for another batch. Combine orange and lemon juices and rhubarb mixture. Refrigerate until ready to serve. Just before serving, stir in ginger ale and strawberries if desired. Serve in chilled glass over ice. Yield: about 12 cups.

Note: If using frozen rhubarb, measure rhubarb while still frozen, then thaw completely. Drain in a colander, but do not press liquid out.

This is our family's favorite drink! It is very simple to make, and doesn't cost much, unless you're in Nome, Alaska. We made it while there, and the cost per gallon was over $12! This lemonade can be spruced up by adding strawberries, raspberries, or other kinds of berries and fruit. An added twist is to make the rim of your glass wet, and dip it in sugar, giving the effect at the bottom right of the page. Compliments a Halibut or Salmon dinner nicely.

Lemonade

Ingredients
- 3 lemons
- 2 cups of sugar
- 1 gallon of water
- Any extra fruit you want to add for flavor

Directions
1. Mix 2 cups of sugar in a gallon of water.
2. Squeeze 3 lemons into the water.
3. Stir thoroughly
4. Mix in any additional fruit if desired. Adding mashed strawberries is a tasty way to spruce it up.

Serve chilled.
Note: Keep in mind the sugar and lemon juice takes up some room, so you may want to fill your container halfway, then top it off when finished adding the sugar and lemons.

Homemade Sports Drink

Ingredients
- 1 cup fresh orange juice (juice from 3-4 oranges)
- 3 cups water
- 1 Tbsp. sugar (or to taste)
- 1/4 tsp. coarse-grain sea salt (Pictured)

Directions
Combine all ingredients and stir well. Cover and refrigerate up to one week. Makes 1 quart.

Try these flavors also!

Cranberry Sports Drink
1 cup unsweetened cranberry juice
3 cups water
1-2 Tbsp. sugar (or to taste)
1/4 tsp. coarse-grain sea salt

Lemon-Lime Sports Drink
3/4 cup fresh lemon and/or lime juice
3 cups water
1-2 Tbsp. sugar (or to taste)
1/4 tsp. coarse-grain sea salt

Ruby Red Sports Drink
1 cup fresh ruby red grapefruit juice
3 cups water
1-2 Tbsp. sugar (or to taste)
1/4 tsp. coarse-grain sea salt

Alaska has more coastline than the rest of the United States combined. Alaska has 6,640 miles of coastline. If you count the islands, it jumps to 33,901 miles!

Orange Chiller Drink

Ingredients
- 6 oz. frozen orange juice concentrate
- 1 cup of water
- 1 cup milk
- 1/2 cup granulated sugar
- 1 tsp. vanilla
- 1 cup ice cubes

Directions
1. Combine all ingredients in blender.
2. Blend until fully combined.
3. Serve immediately.

My favorite Bible verse is Matthew 19:26b "but with God all things are possible."

Alaska is located in the "Ring of Fire." There are over 70 active volcanoes in Alaska, one which we can see right out our front windows! That one is Mt. ReDoubt. It erupts from time to time disrupting Anchorage air traffic. The last eruption was in 2009.

In 1912, the most violent eruption in the past 120 years happened at Mount Novarupta, which created what is now the National Park known as the "Valley of 10,000 Smokes."

Candy Cane White Hot Chocolate

Ingredients
- 1/2 gallon whole milk (8 cups)
- 2-4-oz. packages Ghirardelli white chocolate baking bars, broken up into small pieces
- 1/2 cup crushed candy canes or starlight candies
- 1/2 tsp. vanilla
- whipped cream for serving
- garnish with crushed candy canes

Directions
1. Add the milk, broken up white chocolate, crushed candy canes, and vanilla to a 5 quart or larger slow cooker.
2. Cover, and cook on HIGH for 1.5 hours (stirring every 15 minutes).
3. Serve topped with whipped cream and garnish with crushed candy cane.

Excellent for treating the children after a cold evening out sledding or mushing!

Hot Cocoa Gift Jars

Ingredients
Per Jar (1/2 Pint Size Jar, I use Kerr wide neck)
- Bottom layer- 1/4 cup white sugar
- Layer two- 2 Tbsp. unsweetened cocoa powder
- Layer three– 1/4 cup crushed peppermint candies (candy canes or starlight candies)
- Layer four– 1/2 cup chocolate chips (1/4 cup white chips, ¼ cup semi-sweet chips mixed together)

For Serving
- 1/2 gallon whole milk

Instructions
1. Add the layers down evenly into a 1/2 pint wide neck canning jar. Place the lid on, and decorate if desired. Don't heap any of the measurements or you won't be able to get the lid on. Add a hand written label with instructions.

To prepare the hot chocolate:
1. Crock Pot: In a 5 quart or larger slow cooker, add the contents of the gift jar and a ½ gallon whole milk. Stir, cover and cook on HIGH for about 1.5 hours until warm and everything is melted completely, stirring occasionally.
2. Stove-top: In a large pot, add the contents of the gift jar and a 1/2 gallon of whole milk. Heat on medium-high heat until warm and everything is melted completely, stirring occasionally.

Pumpkin Spice White Hot Chocolate

Ingredients
- 1 cup of heavy cream
- 2 cups of milk – I used skim milk
- 1 cup of good quality white chocolate chips, Ghirardelli recommended
- 1/2 tsp. of pure vanilla extract
- 1/2 tsp. of pumpkin spice
- Whipped cream and additional pumpkin spice to sprinkle on top.

Directions
1. Heat cream and milk in a pan over medium heat, stirring occasionally until hot but not boiling.
2. In a medium sized bowl, pour heated cream and milk over white chocolate chips. Stir until chips are melted.
3. Add vanilla extract and pumpkin spice.
4. Top with whipped cream and a sprinkle of pumpkin spice.

Also try a Pumpkin Spice Latte at The Buzz Café in Ninilchik, Alaska!

My thoughts on "the limo"

The limo was one of those things that wouldn't be, and still isn't, my choice of a vehicle. I have noticed when driving it that it catches mostly men's attention. I would actually prefer a yellow Mustang, because that is what we drove when we were dating, and we have lots of fond memories with it. However a limo is much more practical at this stage of our life.

People are always asking what the limo is about, and if we actually live in Alaska (when we are driving the limo in the lower 48). It seems like we can't go on a normal outing in the limo because someone is always shouting, giving a thumbs up, or taking pictures.

When I do drive the limo by myself, which does happen, I try to be discreet. One time I was at a WalMart in Pennsylvania, and had Shane with me. I was horrified when I heard them announce over the intercom "The owner of a camouflage limo with Alaska plates, you left your lights on". From the next aisle over I heard someone say "let's go out and check that car out and take a picture of it." I made sure to send Shane out to turn the lights off. He said someone was walking in circles around the car checking it out. This made me glad that I sent him and didn't go myself!

It seems the limo can actually detect I don't like it, because it often breaks down for me (It almost never does for Matt). In one week it left me sit three different times. The third time it left me sit, Matt had enough and bought another van. Our other van (the one with transmission problems) was still in the garage, and it was having all sorts of strange electrical issues.

Another time we drove the limo to church, because none of our other vehicles would start. I asked Matt if he would kindly park the car in the parking lot across from church. He parked it beside a semi and it was almost hidden. After Sunday School, while opening the service, one of the ministers said he "noticed the Snader's limo in the parking lot and was glad to have us back." I thought "so much for hiding the limo!"

So do I like the limo? No, not really, but it is better than driving around the old red van with painted squares on the side!

Above: I even drove the limo, with the trailer, to pick up construction supplies. Thankfully I didn't have to turn around! Below: We pulled our little boat with the limo, although even Matt had trouble backing the limo and boat down the long launch ramp.

Breads

Cheddar Bay Biscuits

Ingredients:
- 2 1/2 cups bisquick
- 4 Tbsp. Cold butter
- 1 cup shredded cheddar cheese
- 3/4 cup milk
- 1/4 tsp. Garlic powder

Topping:
- 2 Tbsp. Butter, melted
- 1/2 tsp. Garlic powder
- 1/4 tsp. Dried parsley flakes

Directions:
1. Preheat oven to 400°.
2. In a medium bowl, combine bisquick and cold butter using a fork.
3. Don't overmix. There should be small chunks of butter in the mixture.
4. Mix in cheese, milk, and garlic powder by hand, only until combined.
5. Drop by teaspoon on an ungreased baking sheet.
6. Bake 15-17 minutes, or until golden brown.

Topping:
1. In a small bowl, combine melted butter, garlic powder, and parsley.
2. Brush on top of baked biscuits.

Garlic Parmesan Knots

Ingredients
- 2 cans refrigerated crescent rolls (or biscuits
- 1/4 cup olive oil
- 3 Tbsp. Parmesan cheese (grated, or the shaky kind)
- 1/2 tsp. garlic powder
- 1 tsp. oregano flakes
- 1 tsp. parsley flakes

Directions
1. Preheat oven to 400º. Spray two cookie sheets; set aside.
2. Take the Crescent Rolls/Biscuits and roll into a long, skinny rope. Tie the rope into a knot, sticking the ends into the ball.
3. Place the knots onto the prepared cookie sheets and bake for 8-10 minutes, or until golden brown. Make sure the middles aren't doughy.
4. Mix the remaining ingredients in a bowl, then brush onto the knots while they're still warm.

Golden Sweet Cornbread

Ingredients
- 1 cup all-purpose flour
- 1 cup yellow cornmeal
- 2/3 cup white sugar
- 1 tsp. salt
- 3 1/2 tsp. baking powder
- 1 egg
- 1 cup milk
- 1/3 cup vegetable oil

Did you know: 29,000 square miles of Alaska is covered by glaciers. This is about 5% of the entire state! Some of the glaciers are shrinking, but what you don't hear about in the news is that some are growing!

Directions
1. Preheat oven to 400°. Spray or lightly grease a 9 inch round cake pan.
2. In a large bowl, combine flour, cornmeal, sugar, salt and baking powder. Stir in egg, milk and vegetable oil until well combined. Pour batter into prepared pan.
3. Bake in preheated oven for 20 to 25 minutes, or until a toothpick inserted into the center of the loaf comes out clean.

Grits Cornbread

Ingredients
1 Tbsp. vegetable oil
1/2 cup cooked grits
1 cup buttermilk
1 large egg, beaten
1/2 cup shredded Cheddar cheese
1 1/2 cups self-rising cornmeal
1/2 cup butter, melted

Alaska is home to three different bears: The brown/grizzly bear, black bear, and polar bear. Brown bears and grizzlies vary only in name, a grizzly is simply a brown bear located in the Interior of Alaska. The Kodiak bear is a subspecies of the brown bear, and not a separate species.

Directions
1. Preheat the oven to 425°.
2. Preheat a 10 inch cast iron skillet in the oven and grease with oil.
3. Combine the cooked grits, buttermilk, and egg in a medium bowl and stir.
4. Add the Cheddar cheese, cornmeal, and butter, stirring until smooth.
5. Pour into the hot skillet.
6. Bake for 25 to 30 minutes or until golden brown and firm in the middle.

Bread Bowl

Creamy Gnocchi Soup

Ingredients
- 2 cups warm water
- 2 pkg. active dry yeast (5 1/2 tsp.)
- 1/2 cup butter, melted
- 2 Tbsp. sugar
- 3 tsp. salt
- 6 1/2 cups flour

Directions
1. Pour warm water into a mixing bowl, sprinkle in yeast.
2. Let it dissolve until the yeast gets foamy.
3. Add melted butter, sugar, and salt and mix until combined.
4. Gradually add flour.
5. Once combined, knead the dough for 5 minutes.
6. Preheat oven to 425°.
7. Punch dough down, and shape into six ball of equal size.
8. Place on greased cookie sheet, and let rise till doubled.
9. Bake 20-25 minutes, or until golden brown.
10. Let cool and cut off top, remove some of the bread from the inside and fill with soup (or dip).

Rolls with Strawberry Honey Butter

Rolls:
Ingredients
- 1 cup warm milk
- 1/2 cup butter, softened
- 1/4 cup granulated sugar
- 2 large eggs, room temperature
- 1/2 tsp. salt
- 4 cups all-purpose flour
- 2 1/4 tsp. active dry yeast

Polar bears are the only species of bear that will actively hunt humans for food, although other bears have been known to occasionally snack on hikers.

Directions
1. Put the milk (95-115º) and the butter in a mixing bowl. Sprinkle the yeast over the milk and let sit to activate for 5 minutes.
2. Add the sugar, eggs, salt, and flour. With a paddle attachment for your stand mixer, mix for a few seconds until just combined. Let this mixture sit for about 10 minutes.
3. Switch the attachment to the dough hook and knead on medium speed for 10 minutes. Cover the dough and let it rise in a warm place for 30 minutes or until doubled.
4. Divide and roll dough into 15 balls. You may have more or less depending on the size you make the rolls.
5. Place in a greased 9x13 pan. Cover and rise for 15 minutes. Bake at 375 for 13 to 16 minutes or until lightly browned.

Strawberry Honey Butter
Ingredients
- 3 Sticks Butter, room temperature
- 1/2 cup Powdered Sugar
- 1/2 cup Strawberries, diced really small
- 1/4 cup Honey
- 1-2 tsp. Cinnamon (optional)

There are more caribou than people in Alaska!

Directions
1. Measure all of your ingredients into a stand mixer (or mixing bowl) and whisk all of the ingredients well. Every so often turn it off, scrape the sides of the bowl, then let it run again.
2. Whisk for about 4-5 minutes, or until it goes from clumpy, to smoother, to creamy.
3. Store in an air-tight container in the fridge. For easier spreading, get it out about 20-30 minutes before serving to soften.

Note: Pictured on previous page as well, on top of roll.

Bannock

Ingredients
- 3 cups flour
- 4 tsp. baking powder
- 1 tsp salt
- 3 Tbsp. shortening
- 3/4 cup water

Blueberry Bannock add:
- 1 cup blue berries
- 1/2 cup sugar

Raspberry Bannock add:
- 1 cup raspberries
- 3/4 cup sugar

THIS IS MATT'S RECIPE, AND MADE BY MATT

Directions
1. Mix the dry ingredients together
2. Slowly add water and knead, until dough is between biscuit and bread dough.
3. Shape into a ball, and put into a greased cast iron skillet
4. Set oven between low and medium, and after 15 minutes flip. Before flipping, add grease to top of bread. It is better to bake it slow. Due to variations in ovens, you may need to experiment with settings.

We have made this over campfires as well. That can be trickier, but it is pretty forgiving. It is a popular bread in the north. The loaf is a very stout hunk of bread, but is actually pretty good. Our children like eating it with jelly. The raspberry bannock is our favorite. Note: If you use frozen berries, add less water because the berries will thaw and add more water. Add additional flour if mixture becomes to runny. Warning: Has enough gluten in it to kill a gluten intolerant horse!

Fun with Bannock! On the top: Burned the bannock! Don't despair, usually part of it is edible if this happens. Middle left: Raspberry Bannock, not finished baking. Middle right: Blueberry Bannock, up close. The blueberry variation seems more crumbly than the others, but tastes good anyway. For being a simple recipe, our family enjoys it. In fact, Matt made all the bannock pictured in this cook book! Bottom Picture: Raspberry Bannock, which is our favorite. Because raspberry's tend to be more tart, we add more sugar to the recipe.

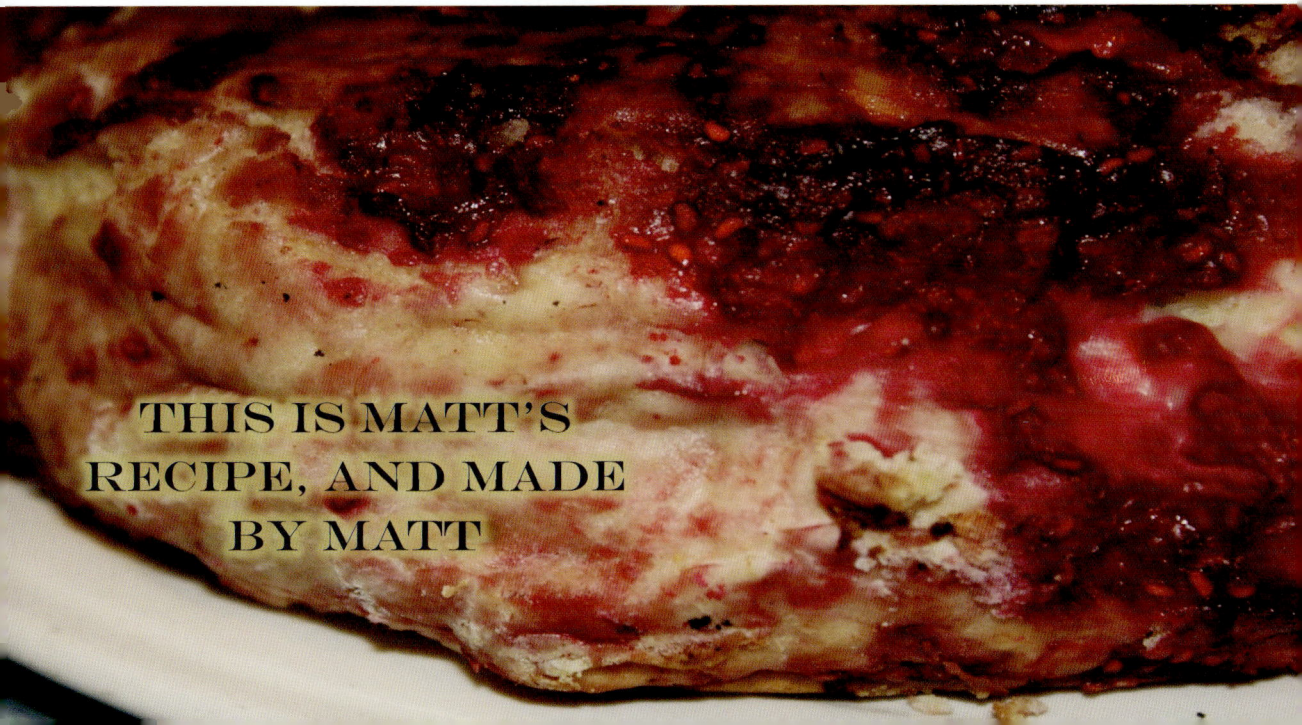

THIS IS MATT'S RECIPE, AND MADE BY MATT

Fireweed Jelly

Ingredients
- 8 cups fireweed blossoms
- 1/4 cup lemon juice
- 4 1/2 cups water
- 2 packages Sure Jell (or other powdered pectin)
- 5 cups sugar

Directions
1. Pick, wash, and measure fireweed blossoms (flower part only, no stems).
2. Add lemon juice and 4-water. Boil 10 minutes and strain. Take the strained juice and heat to luke-warm.
3. Add pectin all at once and bring to a boil. Add 5 cups sugar and return to full boil.
4. Boil hard for 1 minute. Pour into hot clean jars and seal.
5. Process in boiling water bath for 10 minutes.

Note: Any part of the stem will make the jelly bitter. Make sure to only include petals.

How do we stay organized while we travel?

Some people might assume, because we travel a lot, I am an organized person. You can't travel with seven children and stay organized (or I can't). Many times we need to make a quick stop for things I forgot to pack, including diapers, and even clothes, including shoes. There are some tricks I have learned to use while traveling. The girls' hair, for example, can be combed certain ways that will stay nice for awhile.

While driving, once a day, we empty the trash out of the van. There are smashed French fries, drink cans, boxes and wrappers flying out every door by then. This is especially embarrassing on a windy day. Amidst the chaos, the children make lots of good memories and don't mind my disorganization.

Our motorhome has been a real help in traveling. We can keep our trash under control much easier in the motorhome. The children can sit at the table, color, and do school work while we drive.

When we travel, each child has their own duffel bag of things, whether it is school books, coloring books, or dolls. Our children love to read, which helps pass the time. Audio books and music help too. We do have to settle occasional fights, since they actually fight more in the motorhome than the van or limo, because they have room to move around.

The kitchen in the motorhome is very helpful for traveling. The stove can be used for baking pizza or warming food. The refrigerator is great for keeping things like lunch meat, drinks, etc. Occasionally the refrigerator door would fly open, sending mayo and other food across the motor home. It is difficult to cook while driving, so we often make wraps and sandwiches. Even though we pack our own food, we still have restaurant favorites we stop at along the way.

Breakfast

Enchilada Tortilla Breakfast

Ingredients
- 8-10 flour tortillas

Enchilada Filling
- 2 cups cooked and cubed ham
- 1 green bell pepper, chopped
- 2 Tbsp. chopped green onions
- 2 1/2 cups tater tots or hash browns
- 1 1/2 cups freshly grated Pepper Jack cheese, divided
- 1 1/2 cups freshly grated cheddar cheese, divided
- 1/4 cup mild salsa (use medium if you like heat)

Creamy Salsa Sauce
- 2 Tbsp. unsalted butter
- 2 Tbsp. olive oil
- 1/4 cup all-purpose flour
- 1 14 oz. can low sodium chicken broth
- 1 tsp. garlic powder
- 1/2 tsp. ground cumin
- 1/2 tsp. chili powder
- 1/2 tsp. onion powder
- 1/2 tsp. salt (or less if your ham is very salty)
- 1/2 cup sour cream
- 1/4 cup salsa (use medium if you like heat)

Garnishes (Optional)
- sour cream
- tomatoes
- avocados
- cilantro
- chips
- freshly squeezed lime
- hot sauce

Directions
1. Bake tater tots according to package directions, broiling at the end so they are extra crispy.
2. Creamy Salsa Sauce: Meanwhile, in a medium saucepan, melt butter in olive oil over medium heat.
3. Sprinkle in flour and cook for 3 minutes (it will be thick). Reduce heat to low and slowly whisk in chicken broth until smooth followed by spices.
4. Bring to a boil and simmer until slightly thickened. Remove from heat and stir in salsa and sour cream. Set aside.
5. Enchilada Filling: In a large bowl, combine ham, peppers, green onions, tater tots, 1 cups Pepper Jack Cheese, 1 cup cheddar cheese and 1/4 cup salsa.
6. Assemble: Preheat oven to 350º. Spread 1/3 cup Creamy Salsa Sauce on the bottom of a lightly greased 9"x13" baking dish (layer will be very thin).
7. Evenly divide enchilada filling between tortillas then roll them up tightly burrito style, then line them in the dish. You can cover and refrigerate at this point to bake later OR Top enchiladas with remaining Creamy Salsa Sauce and remaining cheeses and proceed to bake.
8. Bake uncovered at 350º for 30 minutes then broil until cheese is golden. Top with desired garnishes.

Raspberry Sweet Rolls

Ingredients
For the dough:

- 2 packages yeast (4 1/2 tsp.), dissolved in 1 cup lukewarm water
- 6 tsp. shortening (Crisco)
- 1 cup granulated sugar
- 9 cups unbleached all-purpose flour
- 2 cups hot water
- 2 eggs, beaten
- 1 Tbsp. salt

For the filling:

- 1/2 cup softened butter
- 1/2 cup light brown sugar
- 3 1/2 cups frozen raspberries
- 1/3 cup granulated sugar
- Zest of 1 large lemon
- 1 1/2 tsp. cornstarch

For the frosting:

- 4 oz. cream cheese, at room temperature
- 1/4 cup unsalted butter, at room temperature
- 1 cup powdered sugar
- 1 tsp. lemon zest

Directions
1. Add yeast to 1 cup of lukewarm water. Stir with a spoon and set aside for about five minutes.
2. In the bowl of a stand mixer, add shortening, sugar, and salt to hot water and beat for 30 seconds. Let cool to lukewarm temperature. Stir in 2 cups of flour and mix until smooth. Add yeast mixture and mix until well combined. Mix in the beaten eggs.
3. Gradually stir in the remaining flour and mix with the dough hook for about 2 minutes. Remove dough from the bowl and place on a lightly floured counter. Knead by hand, add a little flour if the dough is still sticky. Knead until dough feels satiny and smooth.
4. Put the dough in a greased bowl and cover with a towel. Let rise for 30 minutes or until dough doubles in size.
5. Remove dough from bowl and place on a lightly floured counter. Divide dough in half. With a rolling pin, roll one half of the dough into a rectangular shape. Spread dough evenly with 4 tablespoons of softened butter. Sprinkle dough with 1/4 cup brown sugar. In a medium bowl, carefully stir together the frozen raspberries, granulated sugar, lemon zest, and cornstarch. Sprinkle half of the raspberry mixture over the dough.
6. Gently roll up dough into one long roll. Cut rolls, using a piece of thread, about two inches thick. Place rolls into a greased 9" X13" baking pan.
7. Now follow the exact same steps with the other half of the dough, using the remaining ingredients.
8. Place rolls in a warm spot and cover with a towel. Let rolls rise until double in bulk, about an hour. Bake rolls at 425° for 10 minutes. Reduce temperature to 350° and bake for 5-7 more minutes or until golden brown. Remove pans from oven and let cool on a wire rack.
9. While the rolls are cooling, make the frosting. In a medium bowl, combine cream cheese, butter, powdered sugar, and lemon zest. Using electric mixer, beat until smooth. Spread frosting on rolls and serve.

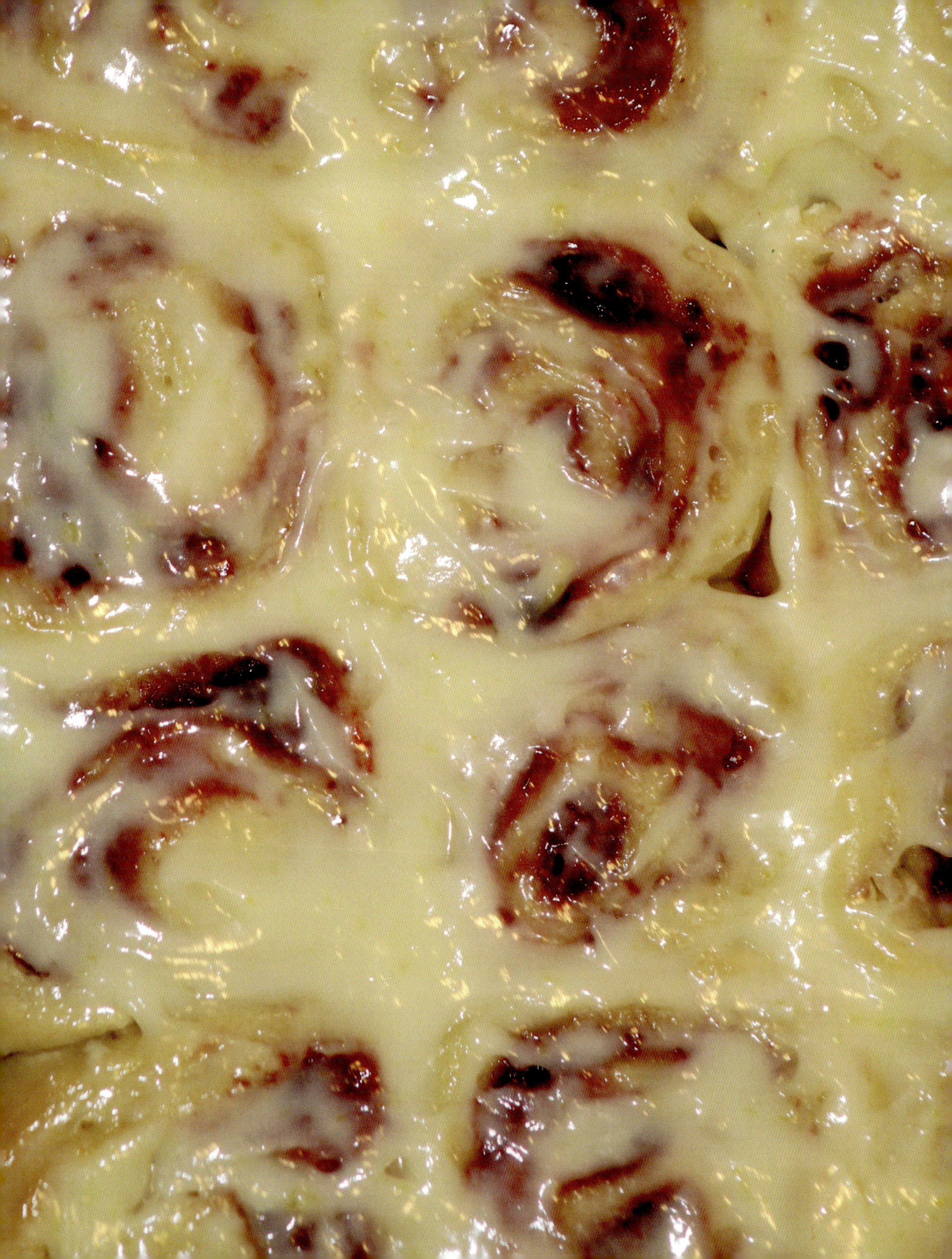

Toasted Oats

Ingredients:
- 12 cups oatmeal
- 2 cups brown sugar
- 4 tsp. Cinnamon
- 2 cups butter

Directions:
1. Melt butter in a kettle and add rest of ingredients.
2. Mix well and spread into a roasting pan.
3. Bake at 300 for approx. 1 ½ hours.
4. Stir every 20 minutes.

We eat it like cereal, works great as topping for parfaits too!

Fruit Parfait

Ingredients:
- Toasted Oats (see above)
- Vanilla Yogurt
- Fruit of Your Choice

Directions:
1. Put toasted oats on bottom of cup
2. Next put yogurt in cup
3. Add your fruit, layered with yogurt and oats

We love this with strawberries and blueberries! But you can use any kind of fruit.

Strawberry Cream Cheese Danish

Ingredients

- 2 (8 oz.) cans refrigerated crescent rolls
- 8 oz. cream cheese, room temperature
- 1 1/4 cup sugar, divided
- 1 egg, separated
- 1 tsp. vanilla extract
- 21 oz. can strawberry pie filling
- Optional: whipped cream

Strawberries do grow in Alaska, but most varieties need to be planted in a greenhouse. They are ready to harvest later in the year than strawberries grown in the lower 48.

Directions

1. Spray the bottom of a 9" x 13" baking dish. Unroll one can of crescent dough into the baking dish. Press seams to seal well.
2. In a medium bowl, beat together cream cheese, 1 cup sugar, egg yolk, and vanilla. Spread cream cheese mixture over dough.
3. Spoon strawberry pie filling over cream cheese. Unroll remaining crescent roll dough over strawberry pie filling (optional: unroll on a greased cookie sheet, press seams well, and then place on top of strawberry pie filling).
4. Beat egg white until frothy in a small bowl and brush over top of Danish. Sprinkle evenly with remaining sugar.
5. Bake at 350º for 30 minutes until dough is golden brown. Cool completely before slicing and serving!

Cinnamon Roll Pancakes

Ingredients
Cinnamon Filling

- 4 Tbsp. unsalted butter, melted
- 1/4 cup + 2 Tbsp. packed light brown sugar
- 1/2 Tbsp. ground cinnamon

Cream Cheese Glaze

- 4 Tbsp. unsalted butter
- 2 oz. cream cheese, room temperature
- 3/4 cup powdered sugar
- 1/2 tsp. vanilla extract

Pancakes

- 1 cup all purpose flour
- 2 tsp. baking powder
- 1 cup milk
- 1 egg, lightly beaten
- 1 Tbsp. canola oil

Directions:
Cinnamon Filling
1. In a medium bowl combine the melted butter, brown sugar and cinnamon.
2. Scoop the filling into plastic bag or piping bag with small/medium sized round tip in place.
3. Set aside to let the filling firm up.

Cream Cheese Glaze
1. In a small pan, over low heat, melt the butter.
2. Turn of the heat and whisk in the cream cheese until it is completely melted and incorporated.
3. Stir in the powdered sugar and then the vanilla extract. Set aside while cooking the pancakes.

Pancakes
1. In a medium bowl, whisk together the flour and baking powder.
2. Whisk in the milk, egg and oil just until the flour is incorporated, some small lumps may remain. Give the filling a quick stir in case the butter has separated.
3. Also if the filling has not firmed up let it sit longer.
4. You want the filling to be thickened, but still squeezable.
Heat a griddle over medium heat and spray with cooking spray.
5. Pour about 1/3 cup of the batter onto the hot griddle and reduce the heat to medium-low. If using a baggie, snip off the corner and squeeze the filling down into the opening. When the pancakes start to form bubbles squeeze the filling onto the pancakes, by starting at the center and forming a swirl. Be careful not to get the filling to close the edge of the pancake.
6. Cook the pancakes for about 2-3 minutes or until the bubbles on top begin to pop and the bottom side is golden brown.
Carefully and quickly flip the pancakes, cooking for an additional 2-3 minutes or until golden brown. Before cooking more pancakes clean off the griddle with a paper towel.
7. Rewarm the glaze if it has thickened too much and drizzle over the pancakes.

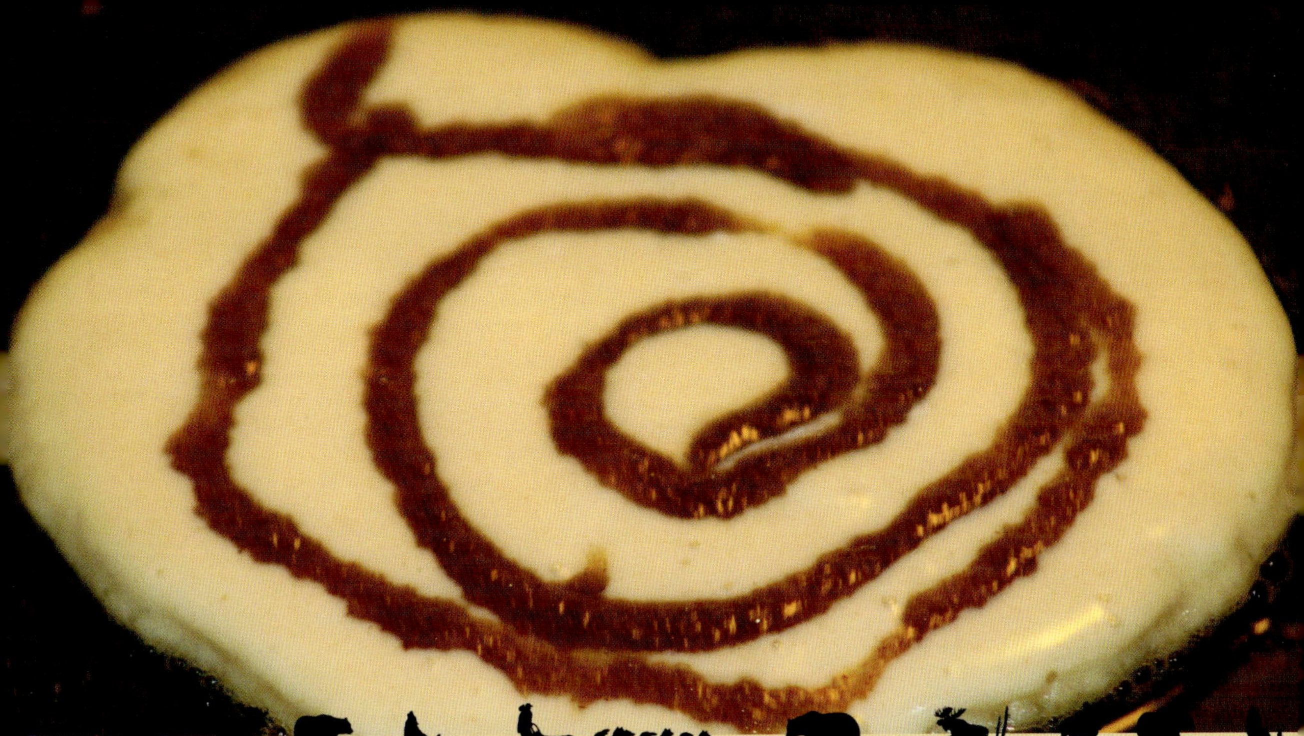

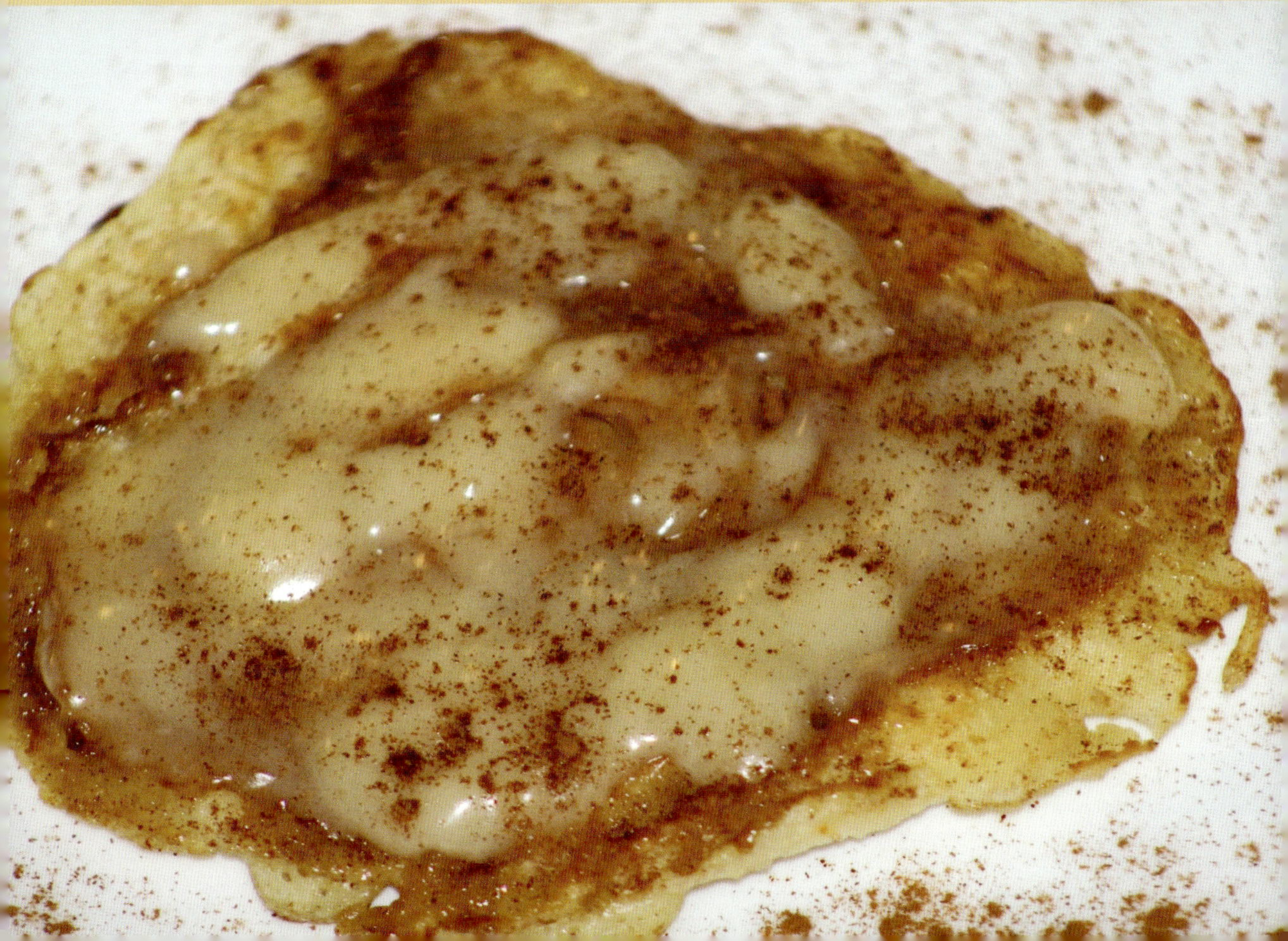

Peanut Butter Cinnamon Rolls

Ingredients

For the Dough:
- 1 package active dry yeast (about 2 1/4 tsp.)
- 3/4 cup warm non-fat milk (heated to about 120 degrees, about 30-45 seconds in the microwave)
- 1/3 cup sugar
- 3 Tbsp. butter, softened
- 1/2 tsp. salt
- 1 egg
- 3 cups all-purpose flour, plus more for dusting

For the Filling:
- 2/3 cup peanut butter
- 1 cup brown sugar
- 1 cup chocolate chips

For the Frosting
- 4 oz. cream cheese, softened
- 4 Tbsp. butter, softened
- 3 cups powdered sugar
- 1 Tbsp. vanilla bean paste or vanilla extract

Directions

Make the Dough:
1. Place milk in a microwave safe measuring cup. Heat for 30-45 seconds in the microwave, until it's about 120º. Add yeast and stir. Let it sit for a few minutes.
2. Place sugar, butter, salt, and egg in the bowl of a stand mixer fitted with the paddle attachment.
3. Mix until the butter is distributed throughout the liquids, although it may be chunky. Pour in the milk/yeast mixture and stir for a few seconds.
4. Add flour and stir with the paddle attachment just until the mixture starts to stick to the paddle.
5. Then replace the paddle with the dough hook. Continue mixing on low speed until the dough forms a ball in the center of the bowl.
6. Spray a large bowl with cooking spray and place the dough ball in it. Spray the top of the dough ball with cooking spray (lightly) and cover the bowl with plastic wrap. Let sit for 1-2 hours until it doubles in size.

Note on rising: if your house is warm, it should rise no problem. If it's cold in your house, it may take longer for the dough to rise, so plan accordingly!

Prepare your Rolls:
1. Stir together the peanut butter and brown sugar.
2. Once the dough is risen, roll it out on a lightly floured surface into a large rectangle, about 12" by 9". Spread the peanut butter filling as evenly as possible over the rectangle, making sure to reach to the sides so the outer rolls have enough filling. The filling isn't very "spreadable" with a knife, so you can place it around the rectangle and smooth it with your hands. Sprinkle with chocolate chips.
3. Roll the dough up tightly from the long end. Slice it into 9 equal rounds. Place the rolls into a 9" pan or 9 1/2" round pie plate that has been sprayed with cooking spray.
4. At this point, you can let them rise for about 30 minutes-1 hour until they are swelling up in the pan and bake as directed. Or you can cover with plastic wrap and stick in the refrigerator overnight until ready to bake.
5. When ready to bake, preheat oven to 350º. If the rolls have been in the refrigerator, remove them and let them come to room temperature while the oven is preheating. Remove the plastic wrap and bake for 15-25 minutes, or until they are golden brown.

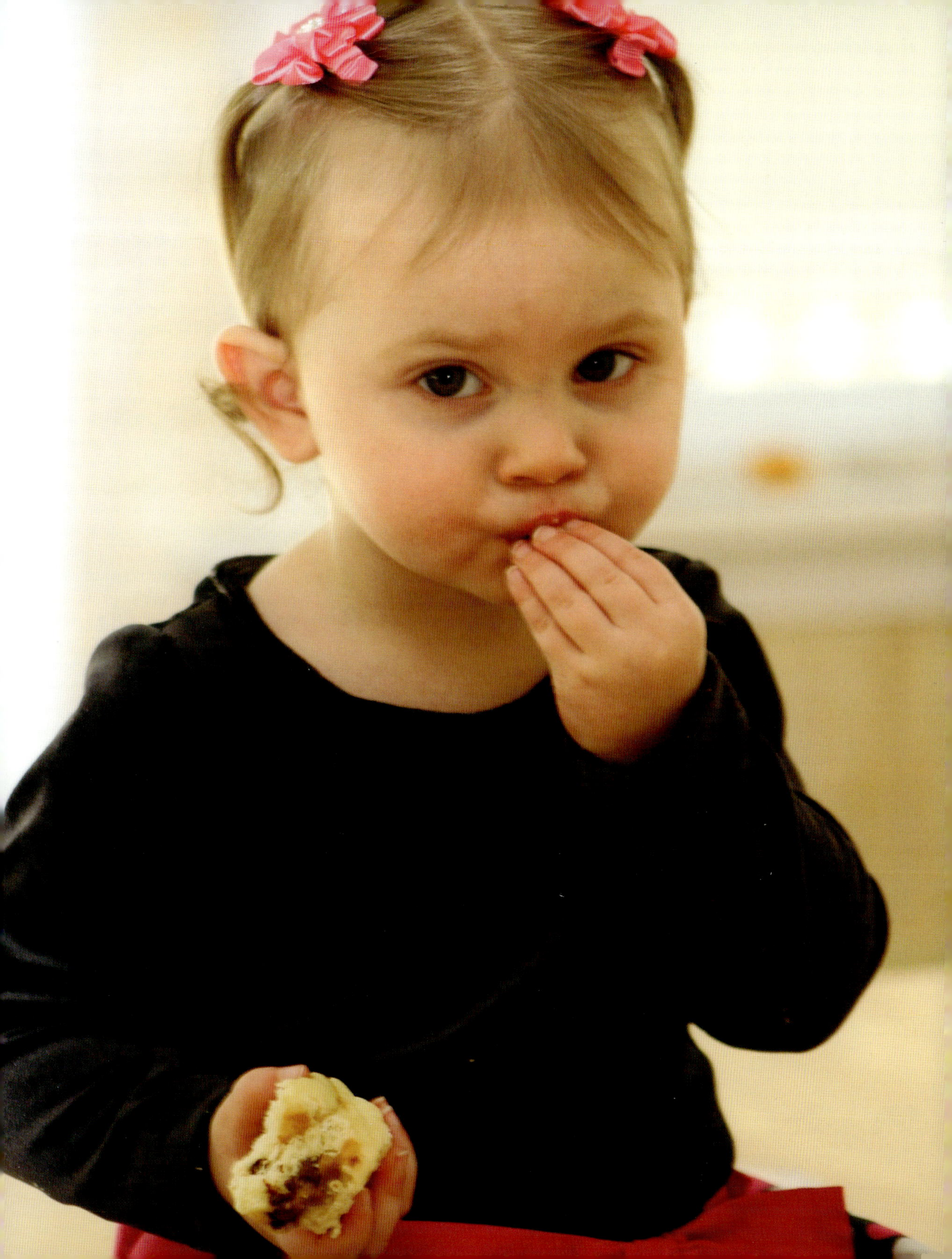

French Fry Casserole

Ingredients
- 16 oz. crinkle-cut fries, defrosted and room temperature
- 1 cup diced ham
- 2 Tbsp. butter
- 1/2 cup diced onion
- 1/4 cup diced green bell pepper
- 1/4 cup diced red bell pepper
- 2 minced garlic cloves
- 1/2 cup shredded sharp cheddar
- 10 eggs, scrambled together
- 1/2 cup milk
- 1/4 tsp. black pepper

Directions
1. Preheat the oven to 425º. Line a large baking sheet with aluminum foil. Optional step to help the fries brown even more: toss the fries in 1 Tbsp. oil (peanut, vegetable or olive are all fine). Bake until browned, turning halfway, about 35 minutes. Once the fries have been removed from the oven, lower the temperature to 350º.
2. In a 9" non-stick oven-safe skillet over medium heat, brown the ham (this helps rid the ham of excess water so the casserole won't be watery), about 5 minutes.
3. Add in the butter. Sauté onion, bell peppers and garlic until softened, 3-5 minutes. Add the pepper.
4. Pour in scrambled eggs and milk.
5. Continue cooking over medium heat, stirring until the eggs start to set, about 5 minutes.
6. Turn off the heat. Stir in the shredded cheese.
7. Arrange the cooked fries on top of the egg mixture.
8. Bake 16-18 minutes until the eggs no longer jiggle in the middle when you gently shake the pan.
9. If you want your fries to be darker, you can turn the broiler on once the casserole is cooked and broil the top for 3 minutes until golden.

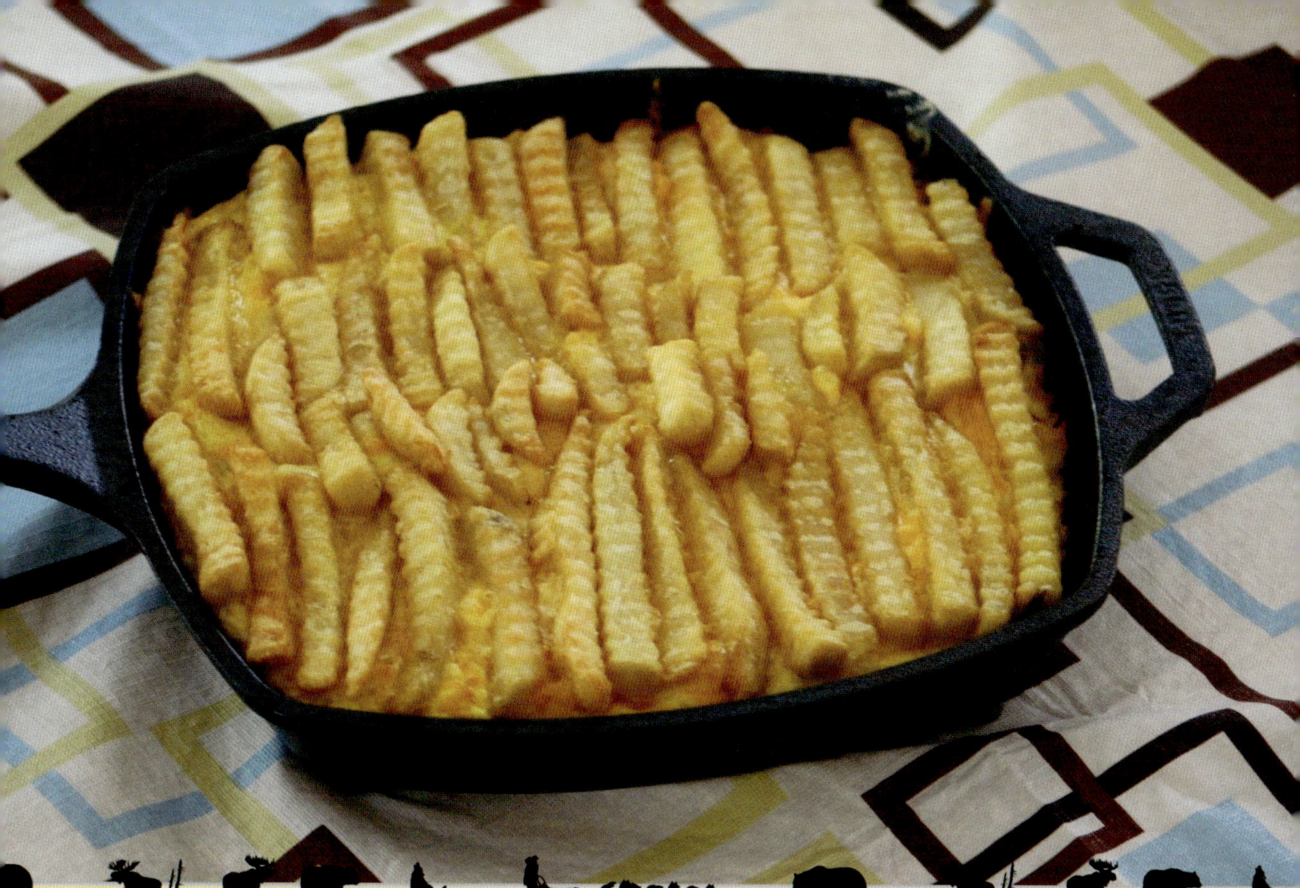

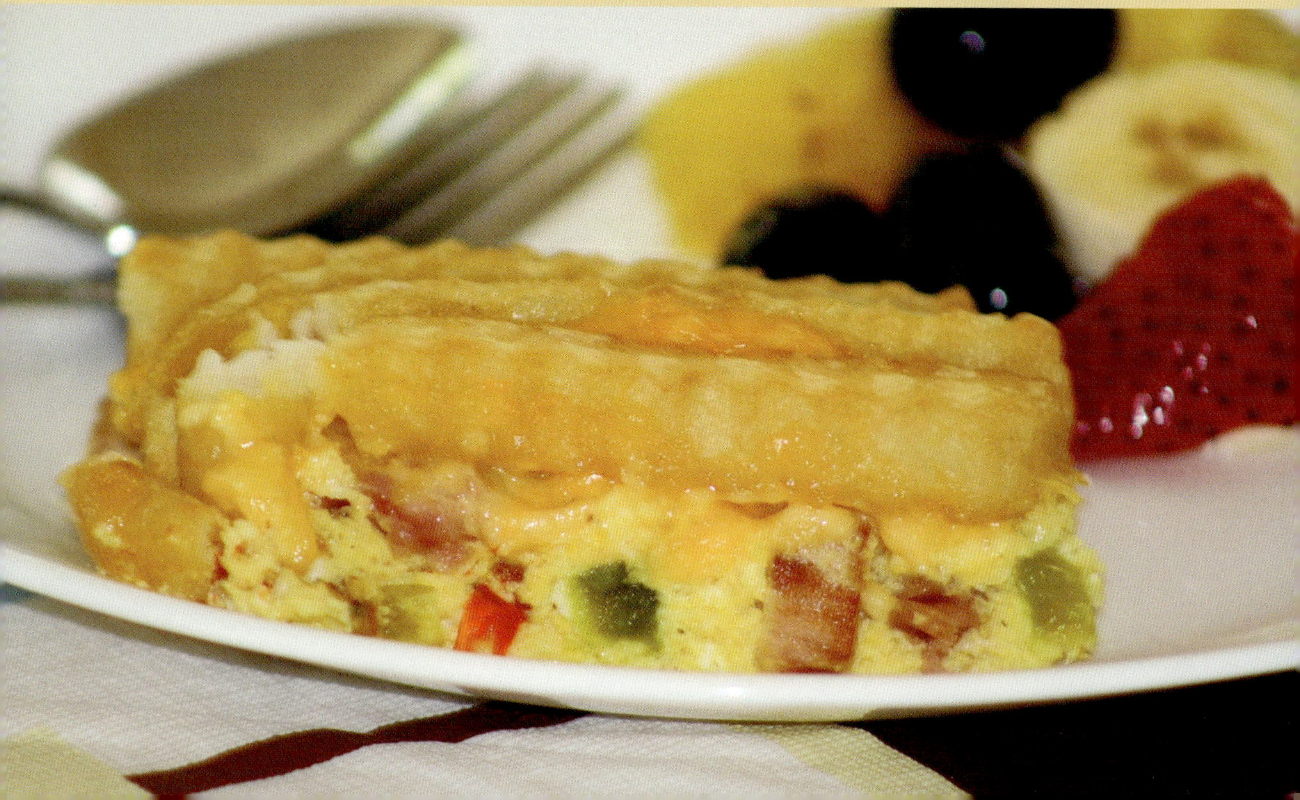

Breakfast Haystacks

Ingredients
- potatoes, cooked, grated and fried
- ground sausage or beef, browned
- green peppers, diced
- hard boiled eggs, diced
- onions, diced
- tomatoes, diced
- favorite cheese sauce
- salsa

Directions
Layer all ingredients together while still warm. Vary amounts according to the amount the number of people.

French Toast Rollups

Ingredients

- 8 slices white sandwich bread
- softened cream cheese, diced strawberries, or Nutella
- 2 eggs
- 3 Tbsp. milk
- 1/3 cup granulated sugar
- 1 heaping tsp. ground cinnamon
- butter, for greasing the pan

Warning! Do not serve these around people attempting to diet. After tasting these, a person may conclude they don't care how much weight they gain from eating them.

Directions

1. Cut the crust from each slice of bread and flatten it out with a rolling pin.
2. Place about 1-2 tsp. of your chosen filling 1 inch from one end of the bread in a strip. Roll the bread up tightly and repeat with the remaining pieces of bread. I really like cream cheese with diced strawberries as one combination and Nutella with diced strawberries as another combination.
3. In a shallow bowl whisk the eggs and milk until well combined.
4. In a separate shallow bowl mix the sugar with the cinnamon.
5. Heat a skillet set over medium heat and melt a Tbsp. of butter.
6. Dip each bread roll in the egg mixture coating well and then place them in the pan seam side down. Cook in batches until golden brown, turning them to cook and brown on all sides, about 2 minutes per side. Add butter to the pan as needed.
7. Add cooked rolls immediately from the pan to the cinnamon sugar and roll until completely covered in sugar.

Cracker Puff

Ingredients

- 2 Tbsp. browned butter
- 2 1/2 cup milk
- 1/4 tsp. salt
- 1/8 tsp. pepper
- 3/4 lb. Velveeta cheese
- 2 Tbsp. mixed onion
- 1/2 tsp. prepared mustard
- 4 eggs, beaten
- 1 sleeve saltine crackers

Directions

1. Heat together browned butter, milk, salt and pepper.
2. Add Velveeta cheese and stir until melted.
3. Mix in onion, mustard and beaten eggs. Put Saltine crackers in 9"x13" pan
4. Pour egg mixture over top.
5. Let stand 1 hour.
6. Bake at 325º for 40 minutes.
7. We normally add some kind of meat as well!

Shane loves to make Cracker Puff, and he is pretty good at it!

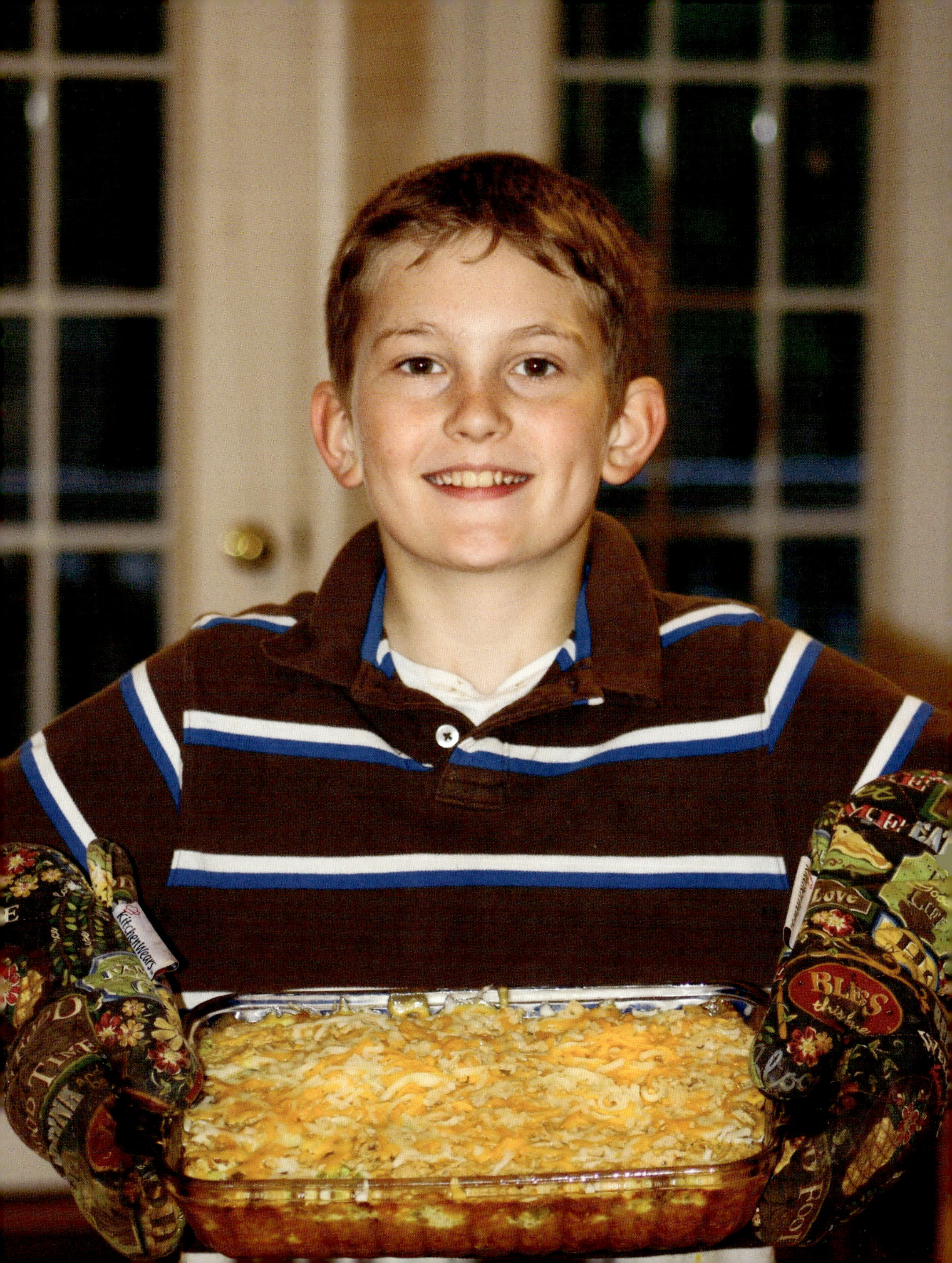

Strawberry Rhubarb Coffee Cake

Ingredients
Cake
- 1/4 cup warm water (100° to 110°)
- 1/4 tsp sugar
- 1 envelope Fleischmann's® Active Dry Yeast
- 1/4 cup sugar
- 1 tsp. salt
- 1/4 cup butter, softened
- 2 tsp. pure vanilla extract
- 1/2 cup warm milk (100° to 110°)
- 1 egg
- 2-1/2 cups bread flour
- 2 Tbsp. butter, melted

Strawberry Rhubarb Filling
- 1-1/2 cups cut-up rhubarb (1-inch pieces)
- 3/4 cups chopped fresh strawberries
- 1/3 cup water
- 2 Tbsp. corn starch
- 1/2 cup sugar
- 2 Tbsp. strawberry gelatin powder

For the Streusel Topping
- 1/4 cup butter, softened
- 1/2 cup all-purpose flour
- 1/4 cup sugar

Glaze
- 1 cup powdered sugar
- 1 Tbsp. butter, softened
- 2 to 3 Tbsp. milk
- 1/4 tsp. pure vanilla extract

Directions:
1. Combine warm water, 1/4 tsp. sugar and yeast in a small bowl. Let sit 5 minutes until yeast is foamy.
2. Combine 1/4 cup sugar, salt, 1/4 cup butter and vanilla in large mixer bowl. Add warm milk and stir to mix. Add yeast mixture, egg and flour. Beat on medium speed until well blended.
3. Spread into greased 13" x 9" inch pan. Brush with 2 Tbsp. melted butter. Cover and let rise in draft free area until doubled, about 1 hour.
4. For the Strawberry Rhubarb Filling: Combine rhubarb and water in large saucepan and cook over medium-high heat until the rhubarb is soft and beginning to lose its shape.
5. Add in strawberries and cook for an additional 2 minutes.
6. Stir together corn starch, sugar, and gelatin powder; add to rhubarb mixture.
7. Continue to cook and stir until the mixture is thick, 2 to 3 minutes. Remove from heat and use a potato masher or fork to mash the fruit pieces. Allow the sauce to cool before readying the cake for baking.
8. For the Streusel Topping: Combine all ingredients in a bowl with a pastry blender until butter mixture is the size of peas.
9. Before baking the cake, gently make small wells in the risen coffee cake, about 1 inch apart. Spoon about 1 tsp. of strawberry rhubarb sauce into each well.
10. Spread the remainder of the rhubarb filling evenly over the top of dough. Top with streusel topping.
11. Bake in a preheated 350° oven for 30 to 35 minutes until the top begins to brown.
12. Cool on wire rack for at least 15 minutes.
13. Combine all glaze ingredients together and drizzle over coffee cake. Best served warm.

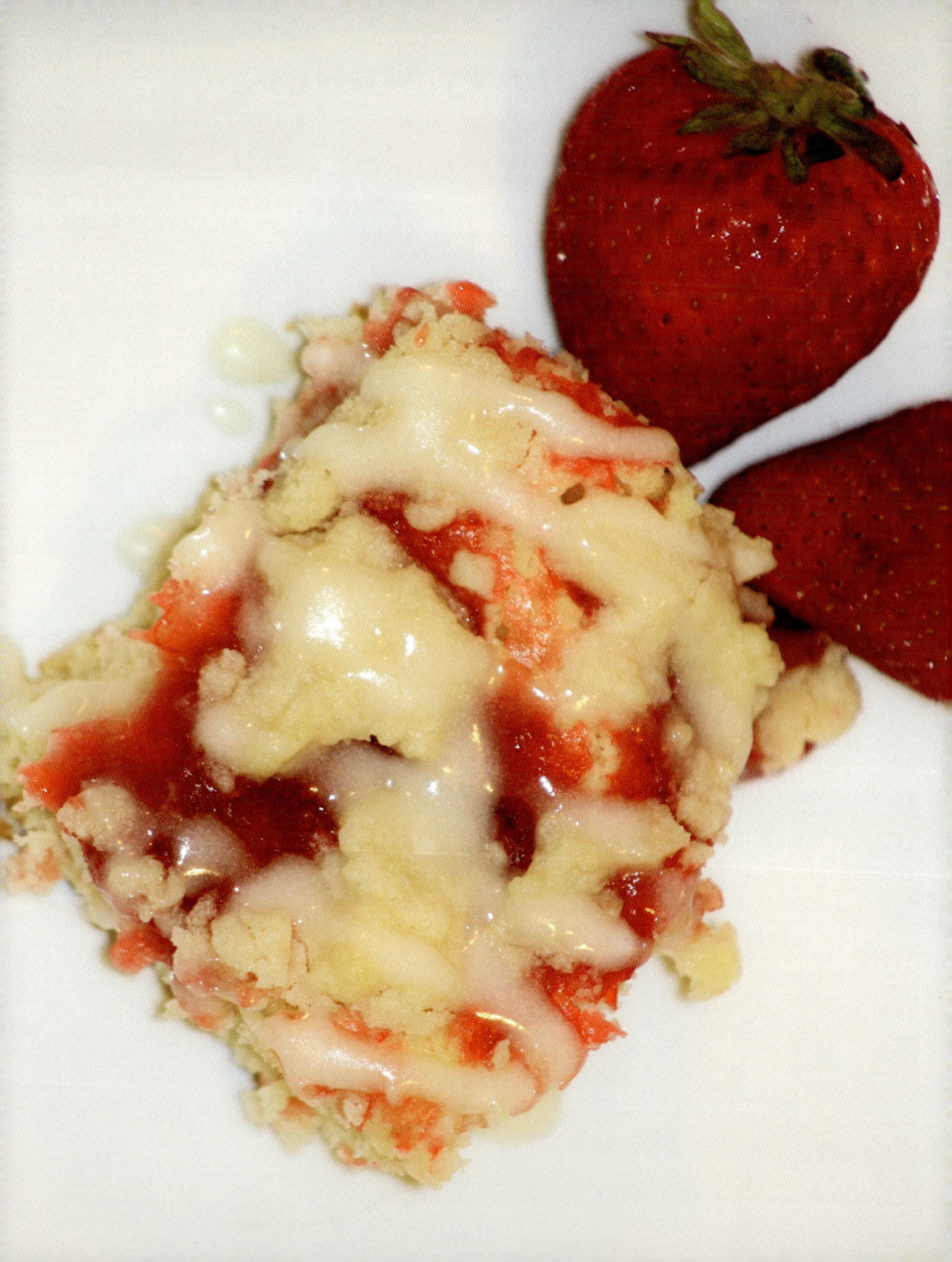

Raspberry Muffins

Ingredients
- 1 cup sugar
- 1/2 cup oil
- 1 cup sour cream
- 2 eggs
- 1/2 tsp. salt
- 1/2 tsp. soda
- 1 tsp. baking powder
- 2 cup flour
- 2 cup fresh or frozen raspberries (or blueberries)

Directions
1. Mix first 6 ingredients.
2. Add flour and mix.
3. Add fruit, do not over mix.
4. Bake at 350° for 15-18 minutes.

Makes 2 dozen muffins

A typical "behind the scenes" picture! Samantha and Mary Kate sample the muffins.

Fabulous Fruit Salad

Ingredients

- 1 medium honeydew, peeled, seeded, and cubed
- 1 medium cantalope, peeled, seeded, and cubed
- 2 cups seedless watermelon
- 2 medium peaches, peeled and sliced
- 2 medium nectarines, sliced
- 1 cup red seedless grapes
- 1 cup halved strawberries
- 1 can (11 oz.) mandarin oranges, drained
- 2 medium kiwi, peeled, halved, and sliced.
- 2 medium firm bananas, sliced
- 1 granny smith apple, cubed
- 1 can (12 oz.) frozen lemonade concentrate, thawed
- 1 package (3.4 oz.) instant vanilla pudding

Directions

1. In a large bowl combine the first nine ingredients.
2. Cover and refrigerate for at least one hour.
3. Just before serving stir in apple and banana.
4. Combine lemonade concentrate and dry pudding mix.
5. Pour over fruit and toss to coat.

Note: You can omit some fruits, or add others.

Soups and Salads

Kenai Cabbage Salad

Ingredients

Dressing:
- 3/4 cup salad dressing
- 1/4 tsp. mustard
- 1/2 tsp celery seed
- 1/2 cup vinegar
- 1/2 cup vegetable oil
- 1 tsp. onion salt
- 1 1/2 cup sugar
- 8 oz. cream cheese
- 2/3 cup milk

Salad:
- 1 quart shredded cabbage
- 1 cup dressing
- 3/4 cup fried, crumbled bacon
- 1 cup shredded cheddar cheese
- 1/4 cup salad topping mix

For salad topping, I use
1 package Ramen noodles
2 Tbsp. butter
Fry noodles, 3/4 of the seasoning packet, and butter till light brown.

Directions

1. Mix the first seven dressing ingredients. Than add cream cheese and milk, mix well.
2. To assemble salad, layer ingredients on a 12" plate.
3. Chill and serve.

Dorito Taco Salad

Ingredients
- 1 lb. ground beef
- 1 (1.25 oz) packet taco seasoning
- 1 medium-large head of iceberg lettuce, chopped into bite sized pieces
- 1 medium-large tomato, diced
- 4 oz. sharp cheddar cheese, shredded
- 4 oz. nacho cheese chips, broken up a bit into bite sized pieces
- 1 cup light dressing

Directions
1. Brown the ground beef in a skillet over medium heat, breaking it up into pieces with a wooden spoon.
2. Add the packet of taco seasoning and stir until well coated. Set aside.
3. In a large serving bowl, combine the lettuce, tomatoes, cheese and ground beef. When ready to serve, add the Dorito chips and dressing and toss to coat.

Dressing
- 1/4 cup ketchup
- 1/4 cup sugar
- 1/4 cup red wine vinegar
- 1/4 cup onion, chopped (or 1/2 teaspoon onion powder)
- 1/2 teaspoon paprika
- 1/4 teaspoon Worcestershire sauce
- 1/2 cup canola oil
- salt and pepper, to taste

Yield: 14 cups

Southwest Salad

Ingredients
- 1 head iceberg lettuce
- 2 Tbsp. minced onions
- 1 cup black beans, rinsed, drained
- 1 cup canned sweet corn, drained
- 1/2 cup Ranch salad dressing
- 1/4 cup mayo
- 1/4 cup salsa
- cheddar cheese, shredded
- 1 medium tomato, diced
- Tortilla chips, crushed

The lowest temperature ever recorded in Alaska was –80 degrees, taken at Prospect Creek Camp in 1971. That's pretty cold!

Directions
1. Tear the lettuce into bite-size pieces and put into 9"x13" pan.
2. Sprinkle onion on top.
3. Spoon black beans and corn evenly on lettuce.
4. In a separate bowl, mix together Ranch dressing, mayo, and salsa.
5. Spread over beans and corn.
6. Just before serving, sprinkle with cheese, tomatoes, and tortilla chips.

Best Potato Salad

Ingredients
- 4 cups potatoes cooked and shredded (cold)
- 1 1/2 cup mayo
- 3/4 cup sugar
- 1/8 cup vinegar
- 1 Tbsp. mustard
- 1/2 tsp. salt
- 1/4 cup diced onion
- 1/4 cup diced carrots
- 1/4 cup diced celery

Directions
1. Mix ingredients together, adding the potatoes last.
2. Refrigerate overnight before serving.

Caesar Salad with Homemade Dressing

Ingredients
- 1 head green or red leaf or romaine lettuce
- 1 thinly sliced tomato
- 1 small onion thinly sliced
- a few black olives
- croutons
- shredded cheese

Homemade Dressing
1. 1 1/2 cup mayo
2. 1/2 cup parmesan cheese
3. 3 Tbsp. apple cider vinegar
4. 1 clove garlic minced
5. 1 Tbsp. Worcestershire sauce
6. 1/4 tsp. mustard
7. 1/2 tsp. black pepper
8. 1/2 tsp. salt

Moose cause more deaths in Alaska than bears. Cars cause more fatalities than moose in Alaska...although sometimes the moose are at fault for the car accidents!

Directions
1. Mix dressing ingredients together then add milk till it has a dressing consistency.
2. Mix salad together, apply dressing.

BBQ Corn Chip Salad

Ingredients
- 1 head iceberg lettuce
- 2 Tbsp. minced onions
- 1 cup black beans, rinsed, drained
- 1 cup canned sweet corn, drained
- 1/2 cup Ranch salad dressing
- 1/4 cup mayo
- 1/4 cup salsa
- cheddar cheese, shredded
- 1 medium tomato, diced
- Tortilla chips, crushed

Directions
1. Tear the lettuce into bite-size pieces and put into 9"x13" pan.
2. Sprinkle onion on top.
3. Spoon black beans and corn evenly on lettuce.
4. In a separate bowl, mix together Ranch dressing, mayo, and salsa.
5. Spread over beans and corn.
6. Just before serving, sprinkle with cheese, tomatoes, and tortilla chips.

Yummy Salad

Ingredients
- 1/2 to 3/4 head romaine lettuce
- 1/2 cup cheese
- 2 hard boiled eggs
- 1/4 cup bacon
- croutons

Dressing
1. 1 cup mayo
2. 1/4 cup milk
3. 1/8 cup vinegar
4. 1/4 cup white sugar
5. 1/4 brown sugar

Directions
1. Mix salad ingredients together
2. Mix together dressing, and serve with the salad

Grape Cloud Salad

Ingredients
- 2/3 cup grape Jello
- 1/2 cup sugar
- 2 cups boiling water
- 1 cup cold water
- 8 oz. cream cheese
- 8 oz. Cool Whip

Adult moose can reach 1,500 pounds. Brown bears and polar bears can reach 1,200 pounds and reach up to 10 feet high, when standing on their hind legs.

Directions
1. Dissolve Jello and sugar in 2 cups of boiling water; add cold water.
2. Let set till syrupy.
3. Beat cream cheese and mix in Cool Whip.
4. Slowly pour Jello in and mix gently.
5. Pour into serving bowl and chill.

Fluffy Raspberry Salad

Ingredients
- 1 pudding (cook and serve, vanilla)
- 6 oz. Jello (raspberry)
- 2 cups water
- 1 tsp. Lemon juice
- 16 ounces Cool Whip
- 2 cups raspberries (other berries will also work, frozen or fresh both work)

Directions
1. Mix together pudding, Jello, water, and lemon juice in saucepan over medium heat until it boils.
2. Remove from heat and pour into bowl.
3. Refrigerate until mixture has thickened (about an hour).
4. Beat until creamy.
5. Fold in Cool Whip and raspberries.
6. Chill about an hour before serving.

Applesauce Jello

Ingredients
- 1 1/2 cups boiling water
- 2 package (3 oz. each) gelatin
- 2 cups applesauce

Directions
1. Add boiling water to gelatin mix.
2. Stir 2 minutes until completely dissolved.
3. Stir in applesauce.
4. Refrigerate at least 3 hours.

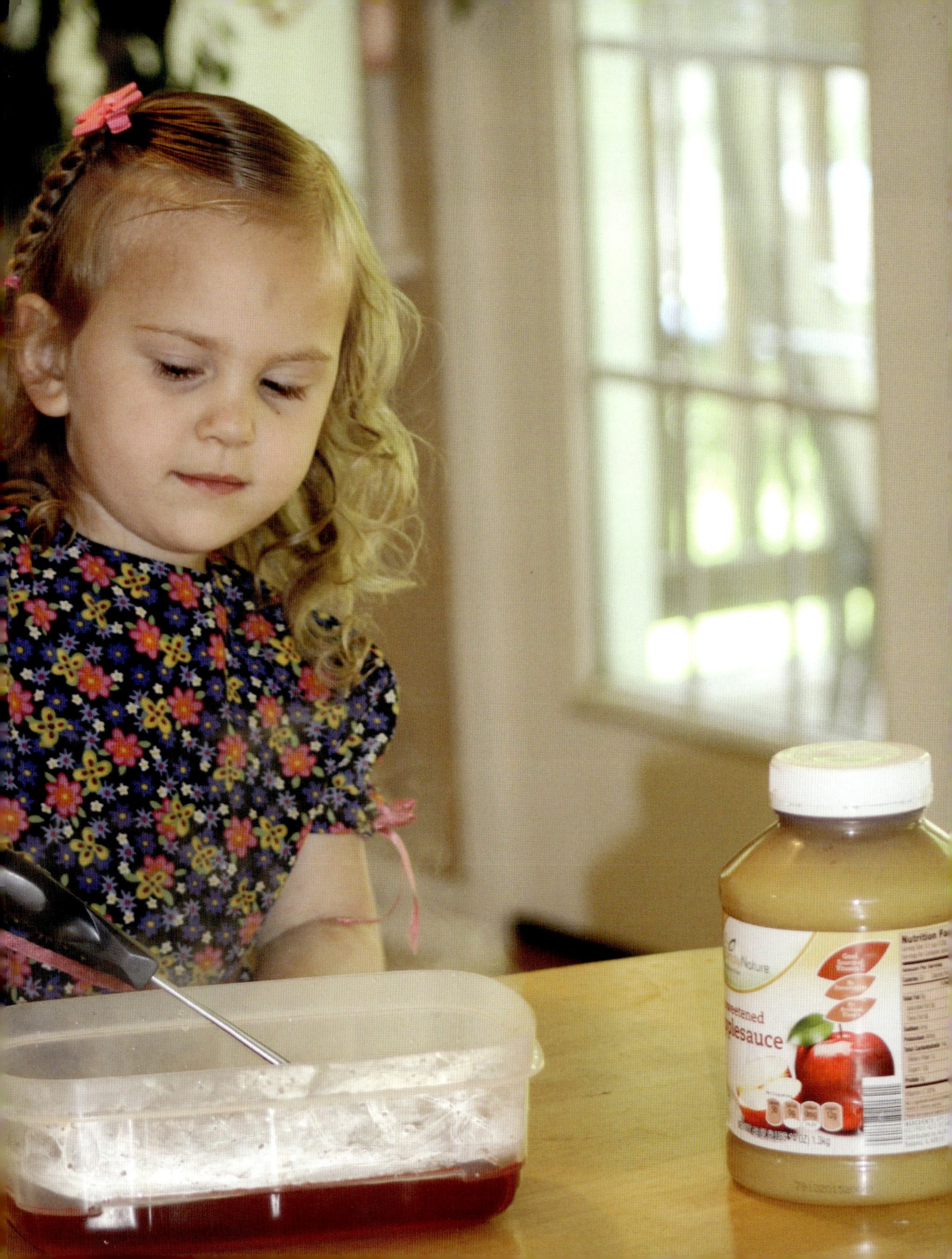

Strawberry Poppy Seed Salad

Ingredients

- 1 cup candied walnuts (see candied walnuts recipe)
- 1 bunch romaine, torn
- 1 small onion, halved and thinly sliced
- 2 cups halved fresh strawberries

Creamy Poppy Seed Dressing:
- 1/4 cup mayonnaise
- 2 Tbsp. sugar
- 1 Tbsp. sour cream
- 1 Tbsp. milk
- 2-1/4 tsp. cider vinegar
- 1-1/2 tsp. poppy seeds

Directions
1. In a large bowl, combine the romaine, onion and strawberries.
2. Combine the dressing ingredients; drizzle over salad and toss to coat.
3. Sprinkle with ccandied walnuts.
4. Serve immediately.

Yield: 10 servings.

A full Iditarod dog sled race team is 16 dogs. Race regulations now require that they have a "northern coat," after someone ran a team of Standard Poodles.

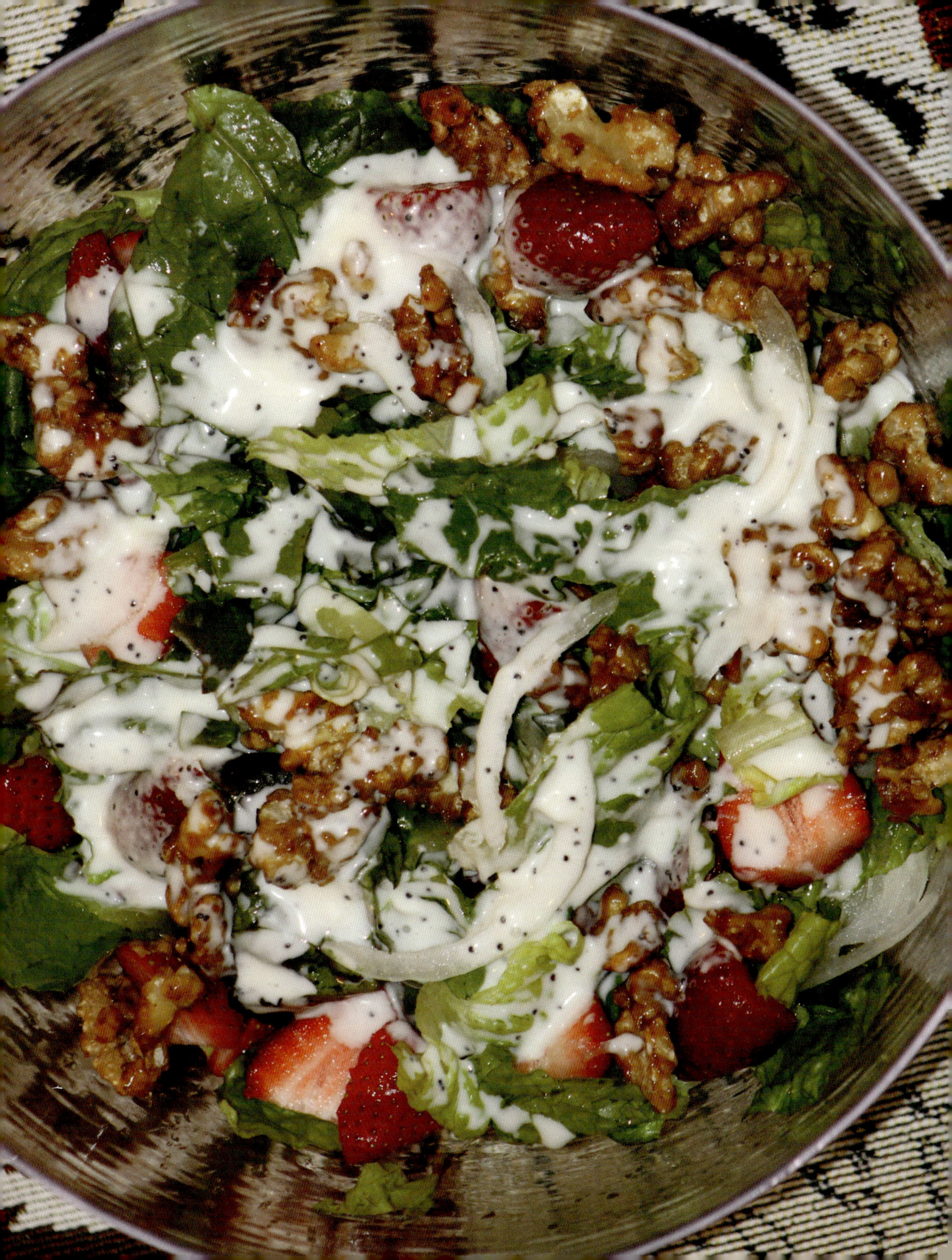

Candied Walnuts

Ingredients
- 1 1/2 cups walnut pieces
- 3/4 cups granulated sugar

Directions
1. Dump your walnuts and your sugar into a pan over medium heat. Stir frequently. After a few minutes the sugar will start to melt and caramelize.
2. Keep stirring frequently, coating all of the nuts evenly. When it gets an amber brown, remove from heat, and dump the nuts onto a piece of parchment paper.
3. Separate with a fork, and let sit for a few minutes while they harden.

Chinese Chicken Salad

Ingredients
- 2 1/2 cup shredded cooked chicken
- 1 bag cole slaw mix or a head of green cabbage
- 1 bunch green onions, white and green parts, sliced
- 1/2 cup slivered almonds (I left these out, I'm not a fan of nuts)
- 2 Tbsp. toasted sesame seeds
- 1 package ramen noodles, smashed (do not use the spice packet)

Dressing
- 1/2 cup oil
- 3 Tbsp. seasoned rice vinegar
- 2 Tbsp. white sugar
- 1 tsp. salt

Directions
1. Mix all salad ingredients together in a large bowl.
2. Combine the dressing ingredients until sugar has dissolved and pour over the salad ingredients. Toss to coat.
3. Allow to set 30 minutes – 24 hours depending on how wilted/soft you want the cabbage.

Most sled dogs are mixed breeds. In fact, no purebred team has ever won the Iditarod.

Gold Miners Salad

Ingredients:

- 1 Romaine heart, chopped small
- 2 carrots, chopped
- 4 green onions, chopped
- 1/2 cup chopped cilantro
- 2 tomatoes, chopped
- 2 grilled chicken breasts
- 1 cup of black beans
- 1 can of corn (or one cup of frozen, thawed corn)
- Your favorite ranch (I made it with a Hidden Valley ranch packet) dressing BBQ sauce for drizzling
- Crispy tortilla strips (I made these by slicing a flour tortilla thin, and then frying them up in a little bacon grease)

The last great Alaska gold rush was in 1899, in the town of Nome, Alaska. In less than two years Nome went from nothing to the largest town in Alaska. You can read about this in our book "There is No Place Like Nome."

Directions:

1. Combine lettuce, carrots, green onions, cilantro, black beans, and corn into a large bowl.
2. Toss with ranch dressing.
3. Place a portion on a plate, and surround with tomatoes.
4. Top with grilled chicken breasts, and drizzle with BBQ sauce. Finally, add tortilla strips to the top.

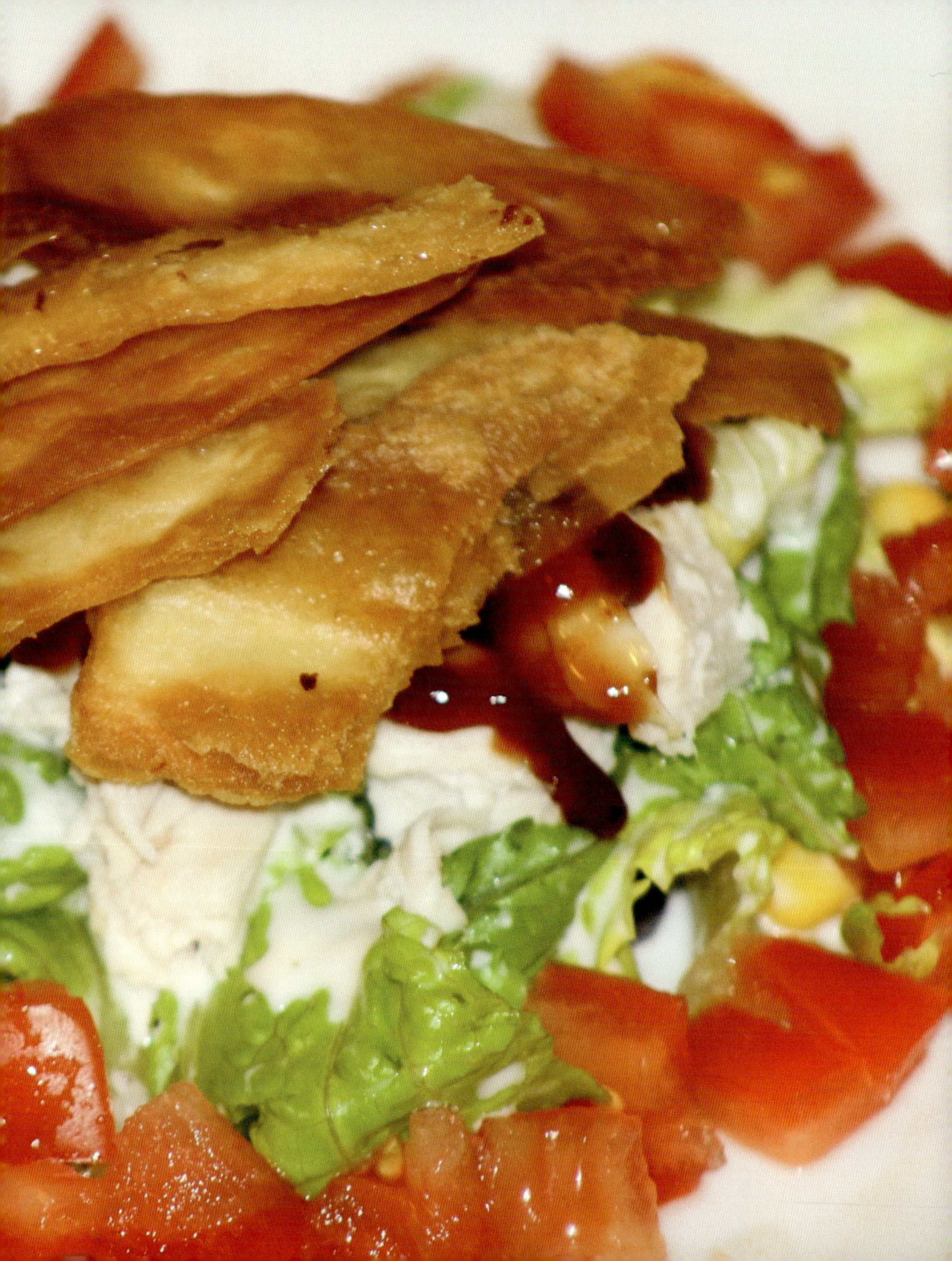

BBQ Macaroni Salad

Ingredients

- 1 (16oz.) box elbow macaroni
- 1 cup mayo
- 1/2 cup BBQ sauce
- 1/8 tsp. Garlic powder
- 1/2 tsp. Chili powder
- 1/4 tsp. Hot sauce
- 2 Tbsp. Apple cider vinegar
- 1 red pepper, seeded and finely chopped
- 1 rib celery, finely chopped
- 1/2 cup cubed cucumber
- 1/2 cup shredded carrots
- 2 Tbsp. Finely chopped green onions
- 4 Tbsp. Finely chopped purple onions
- 1/2 cup Colby cheese, cubed

Directions

1. Cook macaroni according to package directions.
2. Drain, rinse in cold water and drain again.
3. In a bowl combine, BBQ sauce, seasonings, hot sauce, and vinegar.
4. Add drained noodles, chopped veggies, and cheese.
5. Stir to combine, and refrigerate until serving.

French Onion Soup

Ingredients
- 4 large sweet onions
- 4 Tbsp. butter
- 1 tsp salt
- 1/2 cup red wine
- 4 cups beef broth
- shredded cheese

Instructions
1. Slice onions into thin crescent-shaped slices.
2. In a large pan, melt butter over low heat, then add onions and salt, and let caramelize on low, for about 30 minutes.
3. Add wine and broth and cook over medium heat until reduced by a third.
4. Top with bread, then cheese and bake in preheated oven at 350º for 5-10 minutes, or until cheese has melted.

Favorite Italian Wedding Soup

Ingredients

For meatballs:
- 1 small onion, grated
- 1/3 cup chopped fresh Italian parsley
- 1 large egg
- 1 tsp. minced garlic
- 1 tsp. salt
- 1 slice white bread (crusts trimmed), grated or shredded
- 1/2 cup grated Parmesan (optional)
- 8 oz. ground beef
- 8 oz. ground pork

For soup:
- 12 cups chicken broth
- 1 box frozen chopped spinach
- Approximately 6-8 oz. of Acini de Pepe or other tiny pasta
- 2 Tbsp. parmesan (optional)

Directions

To make the meatballs:
1. Stir the first 6 ingredients in a large bowl to blend.
2. Add the cheese, beef, and pork. Shape the meat mixture into meatballs, and place on a baking sheet. I prefer the meatballs to be on the smaller side, but you can make them any size you want.

To make the soup:
1. Bring the broth and frozen spinach to a boil in a large pot.
2. Add the meatballs (uncooked) and simmer for a few minutes, stirring occasionally to make sure they don't stick.
3. Add the pasta and continue cooking at a low boil until both the pasta and meatballs are cooked (approximately 20 minutes).
4. Season with salt and pepper if needed.
5. Sprinkle with parmesan cheese before serving, if you wish.

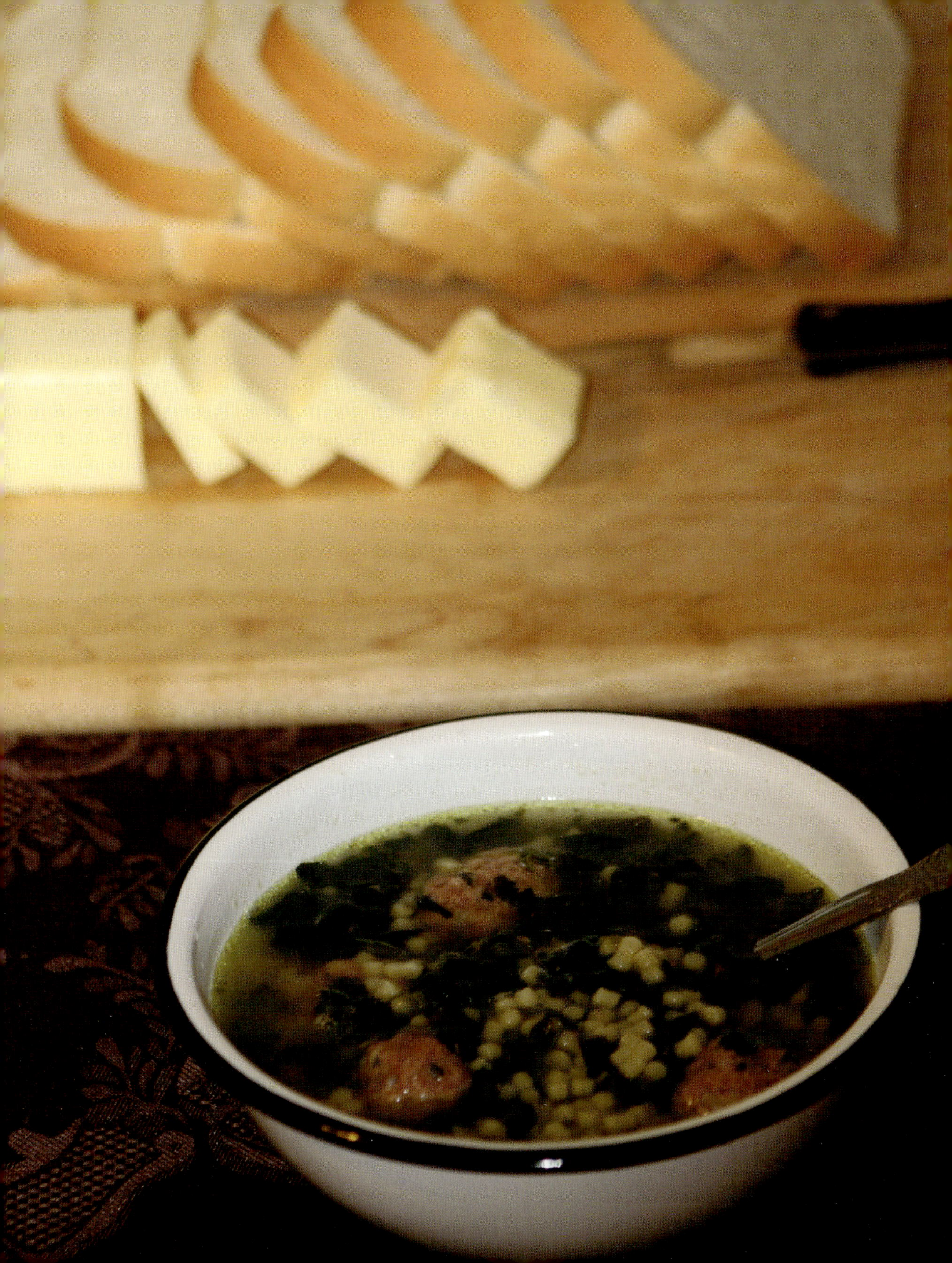

How Do I Cope in Alaska?

The biggest problem with living in Alaska is that our family is not there (yet). Missing birthday parties and family get togethers is definitely the hardest part about living in Alaska. Normally we are so busy building something or keeping the cabin electric and water system running we don't have time to get bored. The fact we need to drive an hour and half for groceries often adds to the running around. In fact, I don't ever remember being bored.

We almost always do things together. This beats sitting around the cabin by myself. While building the cabin, Matt would go to Home Depot and we would all go along. We spent hours in that store, as Matt usually wasn't sure exactly how to do his project and needed to go through all the fittings and connectors. Now if we say "let's go to Home Depot" you will hear a loud groan from the children (and maybe me too)! The upside is we often grabbed a snack or meal at Carl's Junior or McDonalds. Apparently our trips weren't frequent enough, because Carl's Junior went out of business.

Because of our cabin size, the company always stays in our motorhome, otherwise they would probably be ready to go home a few days ahead of schedule! If we get more company than fits in our motorhome, we just borrow a second motorhome or travel trailer from someone at church and park it beside the cabin.

When we have company I take care of most of the meals, although the company often helps out. I like to cook, so I don't mind. In fact we have been getting so much company, some friends of ours bought some land and are planning to build a few cabins to rent.

Creamy Mushroom and Bacon Soup

Ingredients
- 10 bacon strips, diced
- 1 lb. sliced fresh mushrooms
- 1 medium onion, chopped
- 3 garlic cloves, minced
- 1 quart heavy whipping cream
- 1 can (14-1/2 oz.) chicken broth
- 1-1/4 cups shredded Swiss cheese
- 3 Tbsp. cornstarch
- 1/2 tsp. salt
- 1/2 tsp. pepper
- 3 Tbsp. cold water

Directions

1. In a large saucepan, cook bacon over medium heat until crisp. Using a slotted spoon, remove to paper towels; drain, reserving 2 Tbsp. drippings. In the drippings, sauté mushrooms and onion until tender. Add garlic; cook 1 minute longer. Stir in cream and broth. Gradually stir in cheese until melted.

2. In a small bowl, combine the cornstarch, salt, pepper and water until smooth. Stir into soup. Bring to a boil; cook and stir for 2 minutes or until thickened. Garnish with bacon. Yield: 8 servings (2 quarts).

Creamy Sausage Soup

Ingredients
- 2 lbs. sausage
- 1/4 cup onions chopped
- 4 1/2 cup pot. diced
- 7 cup water
- 1 tsp. parsley
- 1/2 tsp. garlic powder
- 3 Tbsp. chicken base
- 8 slices bacon fried and crumbled
- 1 cup heavy cream or milk

Directions
1. Fry sausage and onions in a pan.
2. Fry bacon.
3. Cook potatoes and onions in pot until soft.
4. Add the rest of ingredients together, heat until warm.

Our Schedules with Chores and Homeschooling

We are not very schedule-minded, although as our family grows we are becoming more that way. On occasion in the past, we would leave a day early for a trip. But now it seems if anything, we leave a day late.

When we are not traveling, we do have a schedule we keep with the children. We split up chores into the following: Washing dishes/cleaning off the counter, clearing the table and sweeping under the table, picking up toys and sweeping the floor. The children rotate these jobs every week, unless they do a bad job, then they have to do it for an additional week. The younger ones do odds and ends. Shane is in charge of feeding and watering the chickens. If we are in the motorhome, these jobs continue, except for the chickens. The children don't whine very much, because they realize there is no point in whining, in fact, they sometimes get more work!

Shane also helps clean out the dog pens, and other chores around the place. Desiree is taking a liking to baking, and is helping more and more in the kitchen. Shane is also helping Matt train the huskies for pulling sleds and carts. Shane (and Matt) hopes to participate in dog sled races sometime.

We currently home school using the ABeka curriculum. Lessons on certain topics are covered every day, and then some other subjects are only done a few times a week. We encourage lots of reading, and all our school age children are avid readers. This might be because of the long hours of traveling.

While traveling, we try and teach the children about geography. Our children get to see it first hand, and I suspect they know more about northern Canada and Alaska than most people their age. We like to stop at museums and historical places that we pass. Shane has been in almost all 50 states, and he likes to occasionally point that out. He keeps telling us we need to drive through Oklahoma, as that is one state he has never been. Nothing against Oklahoma, but we don't feel like driving there just to say we were there.

Creamy Gnocchi Soup

Ingredients
- 1 Tbsp. olive oil
- 1/2 cup shredded carrots
- 1/4 cup diced onion
- 1/4 cup chopped celery
- 1 tsp. minced garlic
- 2 Tbsp. cornstarch
- 4 cups chicken broth
- 4 cups water
- 1 package (16 to 18 ounces) potato gnocchi (I used DeCecco brand)
- salt and pepper to taste
- 1/8 teaspoon ground nutmeg
- 1 cup half and half
- 2 cups chopped cooked chicken breast (Rotisserie chicken works great)
- 2 cups chopped fresh spinach

In Alaska, it is illegal to wake a sleeping bear (it is also a bad idea).

Instructions
1. Add the olive oil to a large soup pot set over medium heat. Add the carrots, onion and celery. Cook, stirring until the vegetables begin to soften, about 3 minutes. Add the garlic and stir 1 minute more.
2. Whisk together the cornstarch and chicken broth. Add to the pot, along with the water. Allow the mixture to come to a boil and then add the gnocchi. Reduce the heat to a gentle simmer and stir in the salt, pepper and nutmeg. Simmer for 10 minutes.
3. Add the half-and-half, chicken and spinach and simmer 10 minutes more, until thickened. Season to taste with additional salt and pepper, if desired.

Note: Bread bowl recipe is under the bread section, on page 49.

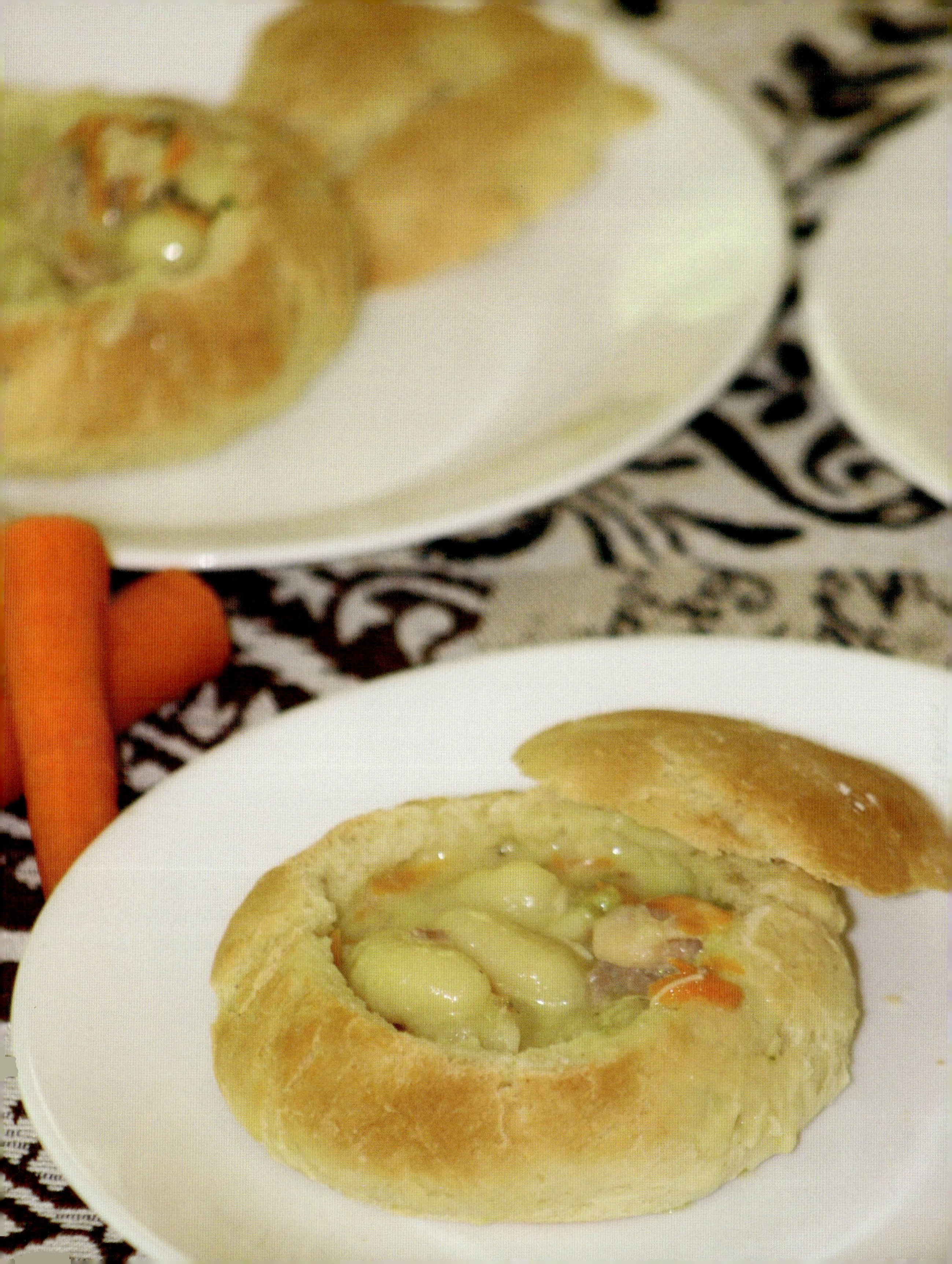

Creamy White Bean and Ham Tortellini Soup

Ingredients

- 3 Tbsp. butter
- 2 Tbsp. olive oil
- 1/2 large onion, chopped
- 2 carrots, thinly sliced
- 2 stalks celery, chopped
- 4 cloves garlic, minced
- 1/3 cup flour
- 6 cups chicken broth, divided
- 2 Tbsp. cornstarch
- 2 cups cooked and cubed ham
- 15 oz. canneli beans, rinsed and rained
- 1 Tbsp. Dijon mustard
- 1 tsp. dried parsley (or 1 Tbsp. fresh)
- 2 bay leaves
- 1/2 tsp. dried oregano
- 1/2 tsp. dried thyme
- 1/2 tsp. ground cumin
- 1/4 tsp. pepper
- 1 Tbsp. chicken bouillon
- 4 cups (1 lb.) uncooked refrigerated cheese tortellini
- 2-3 cups half and half
- Garnish (optional)
- Parmesan cheese

Served with Golden Sweet Corn Bread which can be found on page 47.

Directions

1. Melt butter in olive oil in Dutch oven/large soup pot over medium high heat. Add onions and sauté for 2 minutes. Add carrots and celery and cook, while stirring, for 3 minutes. Add garlic and sauté for 30 seconds. Sprinkle in flour then cook, stirring constantly for 3 minutes (it will be thick).

2. Turn heat to low and gradually stir in 5 ½ cups chicken broth. Whisk 2 tablespoons cornstarch with remaining 1/2 cup chicken broth and add to soup. Stir in ham, beans, Dijon mustard, bay leaves and all remaining herbs and spices.

3. Bring to a boil; cover, and reduce to a gentle simmer for 15-20 minutes or until vegetables are tender.

4. Add tortellini and boil for 1-2 minutes or until cooked.

5. Stir in half and half, adding additional half and half or broth if desired for a less "chunky" soup and warm through.

6. Garnish individual servings with fresh parsley and Parmesan cheese if desired.

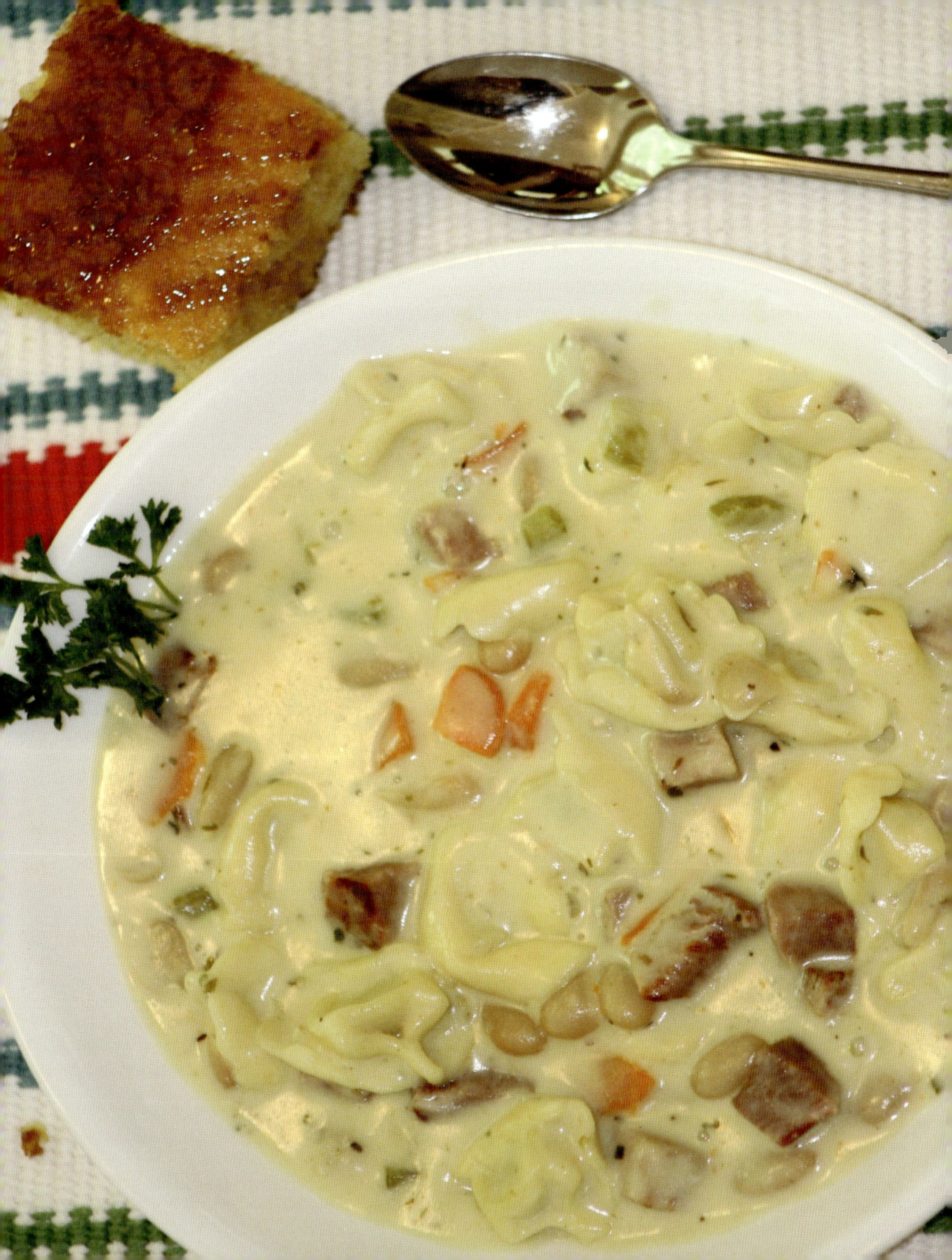

Gardening in Alaska

People often ask about gardening in Alaska. We tried our hand at gardening. We planted cucumbers, tomatoes, cauliflower, broccoli, potatoes, and some pumpkins. Most Alaskans plan their garden June 1st, as before that you run the chance of frost. Many people use greenhouses in Alaska; with one you can raise about anything. We did not have a greenhouse, just a makeshift plastic thing over the tomatoes.

Our garden was a dramatic failure. Everything came up, but the corn got no higher than four inches. The moose ate more from our garden than we did. The broccoli and the cauliflower were doing very nicely, until the moose took off with them. At first we blamed the chickens running loose, but then we noticed huge moose tracks in the garden.

The potatoes actually did okay, and we had several meals from them. The chickens ate some of our other plants.

Matt put a strand of wire around the entire garden, but it wasn't enough to keep the moose out. In fact, it didn't seem to help one bit.

This year (2016) we didn't do anything with a garden, but next year we would like to have a greenhouse and a garden with a large moose fence.

It is possible to have very lush gardens in Alaska, it just takes a little bit more work. The growing season is much shorter, but because of the long sunlight hours in the summer, plants grow faster. The extra sunlight makes carrots sweeter and pumpkins, cabbage, etc bigger.

Also, I don't know if this counts as gardening, but there are a lot of wild berries that grow in the muskeg. Wild blueberries, cloud berries, and many more. The fireweed, which grows in massive amounts covering acres, is also good to eat, and can be made into jams and syrup (see fireweed jelly recipe on page 54). You can have plenty of cheap, fresh food to eat in Alaska, if you are willing to work for it.

Below: Marvin Schrock's greenhouse in Sterling, Alaska

Stuffed Pepper Soup

Ingredients

- 1 lb. ground beef
- 1 small onion, diced
- 1 large bell pepper, diced
- 1 can (29 oz.) diced tomatoes
- 1 (10 oz.) can tomato soup (or tomato sauce)
- 1 (14 oz.) can chicken broth (or beef broth)
- 2 cups cooked rice
- 1 Tbsp. sugar
- 1 tsp. garlic powder
- salt and pepper, to taste
- shredded cheddar cheese, for topping

Directions

1. In a large pot, brown and crumble ground beef along with diced green peppers and onion over medium-high heat.
2. When cooked, drain excess grease from beef mixture.
3. Put beef back into pot. Add in diced tomatoes.
4. Add in chicken broth (or beef broth, if using)
5. Add in can of tomato soup or tomato sauce
6. Give it all a good stir. Then add in rice.
7. Add seasonings; sugar, garlic powder, salt and pepper (to taste).
8. Cook, then add shredded cheese before serving.

So what do I actually think of Alaska?

People often ask me, "What do you actually think of Alaska?" I actually did make the comment "I could live in Alaska" while we were first visiting Alaska, without giving it a second thought that this might actually happen. For me, Alaska is like living anywhere else. Living off the grid I do find annoying, unless the system actually works. We did purchase 80 acres closer to Soldotna, and we are excited to build a nice, normal house that will be connected to the electrical grid. The house construction is underway as of writing this book, and plans are to finish it in 2017.

Without Matt's influence would I just pack up and move to Alaska? No, I certainly would not have! Not because Alaska is not nice, but because I don't like change. I find it hard to get to know new people, and fit into a new community.

I do really enjoy Alaska and all its scenery and wildlife. Even though I'm not really an outdoors person, one of my greater memories is taking the entire family out on the four wheelers and cruising around the Alaska countryside and on the beach. Friends and family visiting are also a big highlight.

Visiting places in Alaska, such as Nome, is still exciting and enjoyable for me. There are many remote villages and towns in Alaska, that we would enjoy visiting. Many of these towns are rather dark and full of lost people, who need the Gospel. While in Nome, one lady, who smelled of alcohol, asked Matt for a hug. Matt declined, but suggested I give her a hug, which she accepted. Another random lady on the street walked up and declared she had an abortion many years ago. On the front porch of our motel in Nome Matt talked to a fellow who said he didn't have anything to do all day but drink. There is no shortage of lost souls that need Christ.

During some of the rough, early cabin times, Alaska almost, or did, lose its appeal. Thankfully Matt has made many improvements to the cabin's electric and water systems, making it bearable. I must say the new house I find much more exciting than the cabin. Alaska looks better every day....

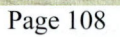

YOU ARE NOW ENTERING THE
WORLD FAMOUS
LASKA HIGHWAY
DAWSON CREEK B.C.
To
Fort St John

Meats and Main Dishes

Mexican Stuffed Pepper

Ingredients
- 6 medium green or sweet red pepper
- 1 lb. ground beef
- 1/3 cup chopped onion
- 1/3 cup chopped celery
- 3 cups cooked rice
- 1-1/4 cups salsa, divided
- 1 Tbsp. chopped green chilies
- 2 tsp. chili powder
- 1/4 tsp. salt
- 1 cup (4 ounces) Mexican cheese blend

Directions
1. Cut tops off peppers and discard; remove seeds. In a Dutch oven or large kettle, cook peppers in boiling water for 3-5 minutes. Drain and rinse in cold water; set aside.
2. In a nonstick skillet, cook the beef, onion and celery over medium heat until meat is no longer pink; drain. Stir in the rice, 1 cup salsa, chilies, chili powder and salt. Spoon into peppers.
3. Place in a 13"x9" baking dish coated with cooking spray. Add 1/4 cup water to dish. Cover and bake at 350° for 45-50 minutes or until heated through. Uncover; sprinkle with cheese and top with remaining salsa. Bake 2-3 minutes longer or until cheese is melted. Yield: 6 servings.

Bacon Wrapped Meatloaf

Ingredients

- 1 medium sized onion, diced
- 2 cloves garlic, minced
- 1 tablespoon butter
- 1 1/2 pounds ground beef
- 1 large egg
- 1 cup bread crumbs
- 1 cup milk
- 1 Tbsp. Worcestershire sauce
- 1 tsp. thyme
- 6 Bacon slices
- 1/2 cup ketchup
- 1 Tbsp. brown sugar
- 1 Tbsp. mustard
- 1/2 cup fried onion pieces

Directions

1. Preheat oven or grill to 350º. Line a baking sheet with foil for easy clean up.
2. Melt butter in sauté pan over medium heat. Cook onions until fragrant and slightly brown while stirring occasionally, about 3-5 minutes. Reduce heat to low and add garlic, cook for 2-3 minutes. Remove from heat.
3. In large bowl, combine ground beef, egg, bread crumbs, milk, Worcestershire sauce, thyme, and cooked onions and garlic. Use hands to mix well, but try not to over work the meat. Divide into six equal sized portions.
4. Wrap bacon slices around edge of disks. Diameter of meatloaf should be so that the bacon ends just meet or slightly overlap.
5. In a separate bowl, combine ketchup with mustard and brown sugar. Divide equally and spread over the tops of the mini meatloaves. Sprinkle tops with crispy fried onions.
6. Bake in preheated oven or grill until bacon is just golden, about 1 hour and 15 minutes.

    It is possible to cook these over a campfire in an iron skillet, but if you do, make sure to clean up. Bacon and hamburger will attract bears! Don't store leftovers in your tent. And if you go the campfire route, your meatloaf probably won't look as nice and neat as an oven-baked one.

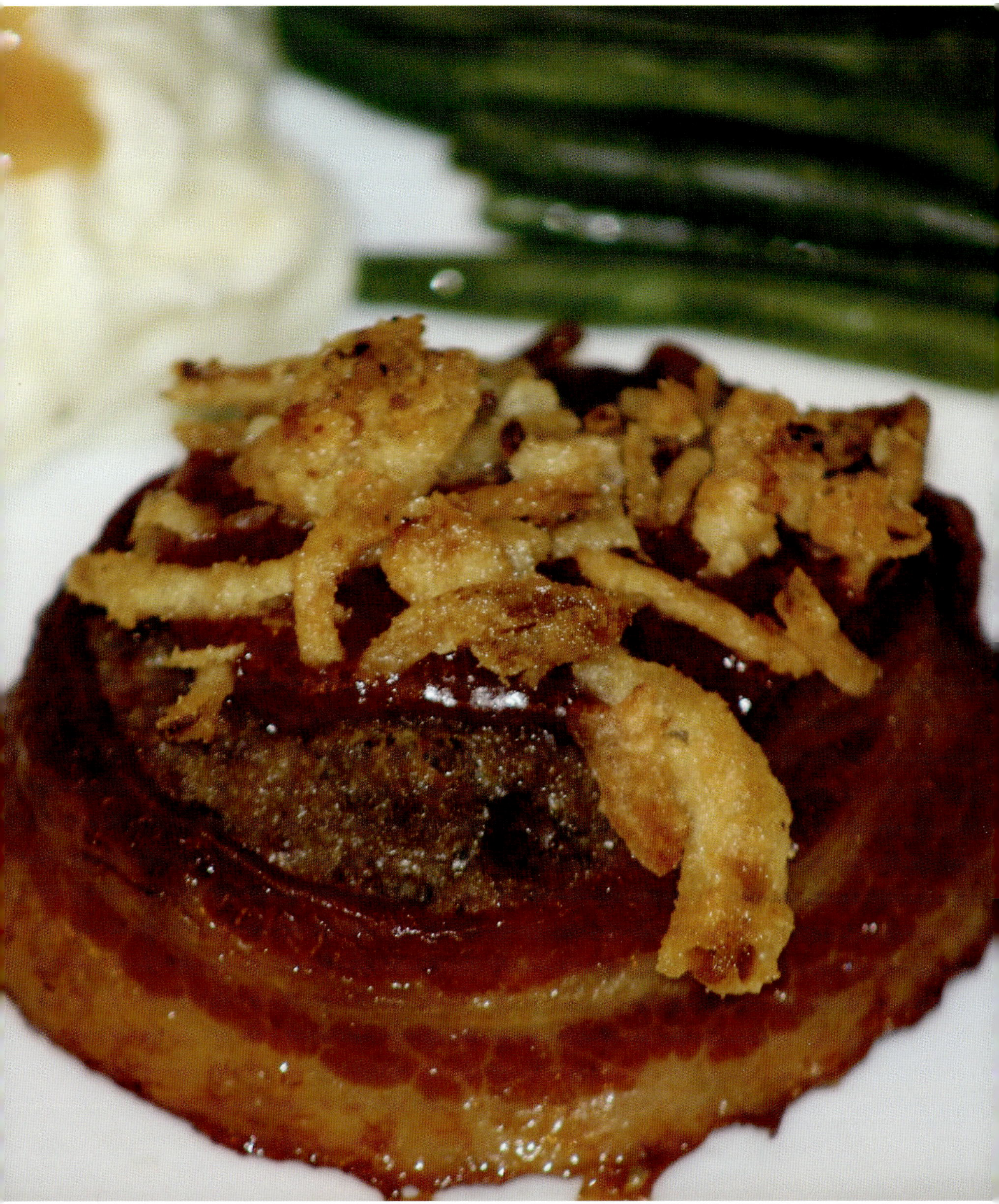

Almost Lasagna

Ingredients

- 2 lbs. ground beef, sausage or moose
- 2 cups thick spaghetti sauce
- 1 cup chopped onion (may fry with meat)
- 1 tsp. salt
- 1/4 tsp. pepper
- 4 oz. cream cheese
- 1 cup sour cream
- 1 cup cottage cheese
- 8 oz. cooked noodles (any small pasta works well)
- 1 cup grated cheddar cheese

Directions

1. Stir beef, sauce, and seasonings together. Set aside.
2. Beat cream cheese, sour cream, and cottage cheese well.
3. In a 3 quart greased casserole dish (or foil pans for freezer) layer half the noodles, half the beef mixture, and half the cheese mixture.
4. Repeat.
5. Top with grated cheddar cheese.
6. Sprinkle with parsley.
7. Bake at 350° for 35-40 minutes.

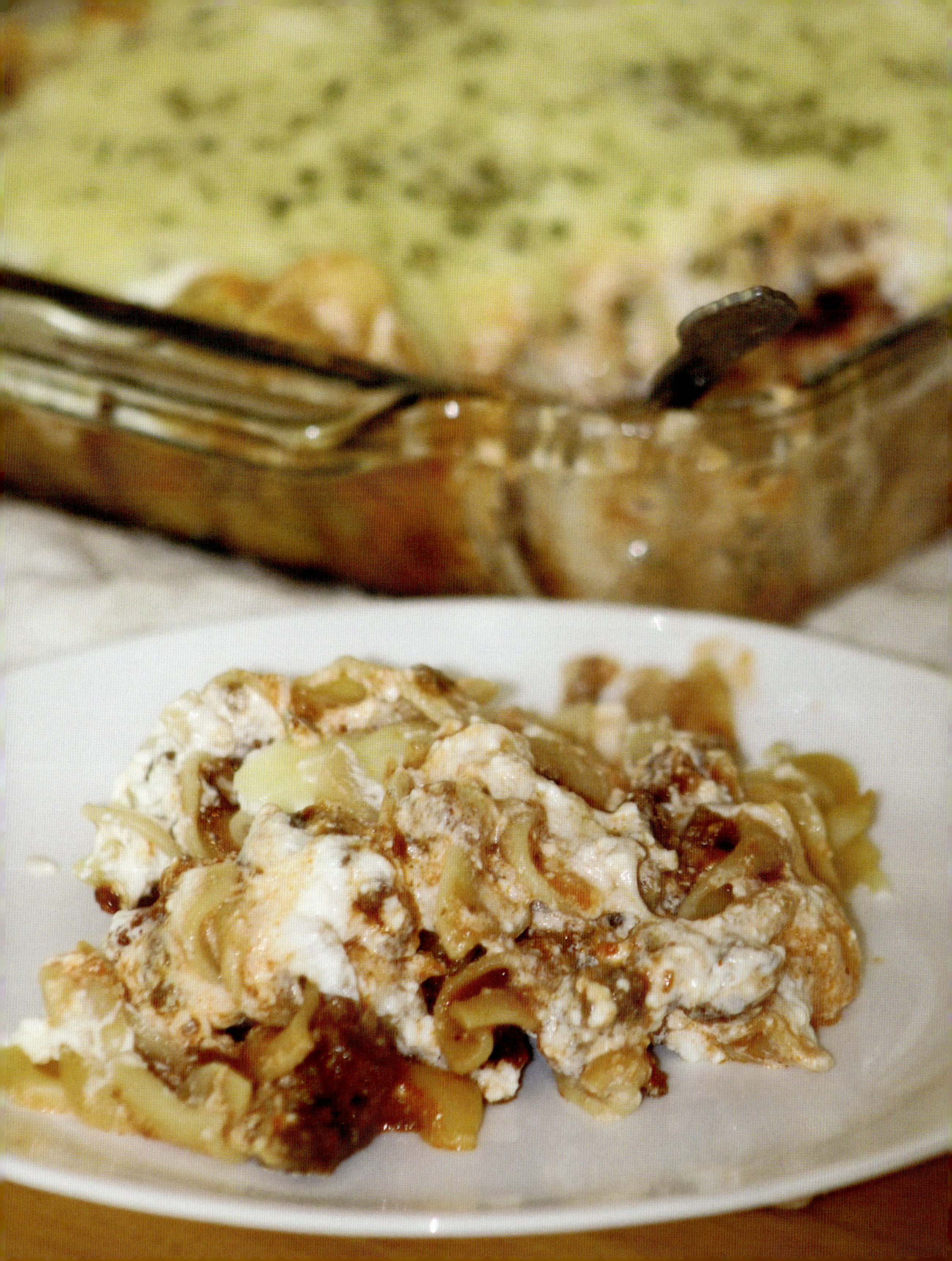

Grizzly Bear Burgers

Our neighbor, Richard, gave us some grizzly bear burger (as of yet, Matt has not shot one), and we decided to sample it. This was the same Richard that was on the fated ship the *El Dan*, in *Alaska Sea Escapes*. Most brown and grizzly bear meat is not considered very good to eat, but we decided to give it a try. It was okay, but tasted a little bit like pork past it's prime. We also tried this burger recipe with moose meat, and the results were excellent. Ground beef can also be used with satisfying results.

Ingredients

- 1 lb. ground grizzly bear (black bear, moose or beef work too)
- 2 Tbsp. finely chopped onion
- 1 Tbsp. mayo
- 1/4 cup dry bread crumbs
- 1 egg, slightly beaten
- 2 cubes beef bouillon, crushed
- 1/4 tsp. pepper
- bacon
- Cheese (your choice)

Lana's Favorite

Directions

1. In a large bowl, mix all ingredients together
2. Form into patties
3. Put patties on a cookie sheet and place in freezer for an hour
4. Grill patties to taste, we prefer them medium. Add cheese two minutes before removing patties from grill.
5. Add fried bacon, to your taste. We like 2 pieces on a patty.

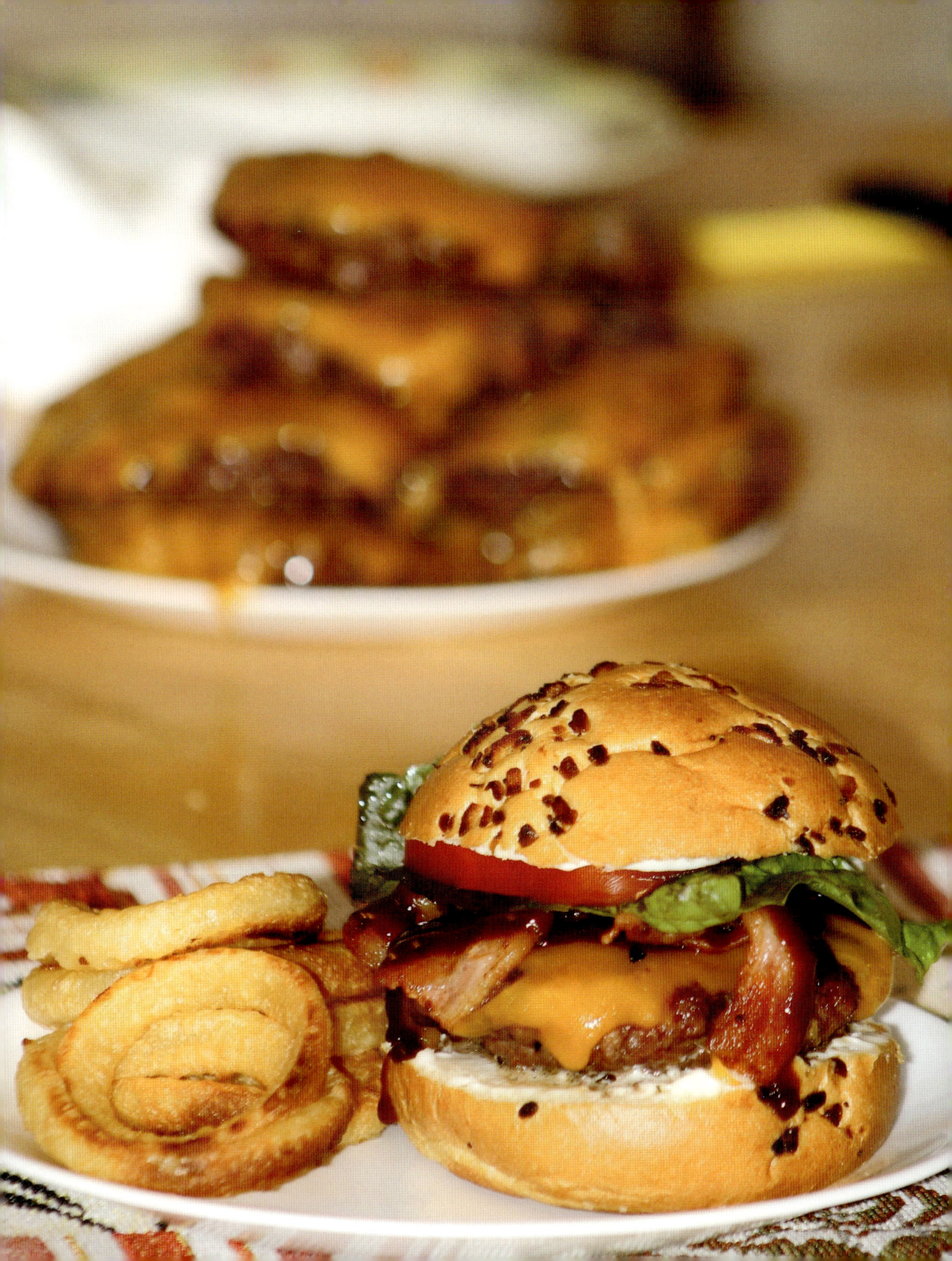

Mongolian Beef

Ingredients
- 1 lb. of flank steak, thinly sliced crosswise 1/4 cup of cornstarch
- 3 tsp. of canola or vegetable oil
- 1/2 tsp. of grated ginger (about 1/2 inch piece)
- 1 Tbsp. of chopped garlic (about 2 -3 large cloves)
- 1/2 cup of water
- 1/2 cup of soy sauce
- 1/2 -3/4 cup brown sugar
- 1/2 tsp. of red pepper flakes
- 3 large green onions, sliced crosswise into thirds

Directions

1. Prepare the meat:

First, make sure the steak slices are dry (pat them dry) and mix them with the corn starch. Using your hands or a spoon, move them around to make sure all pieces are coated. Place beef slices in a strainer and shake off excess corn starch.

2. Make the sauce:

Heat half of the oil in a large wok at medium-high and add the garlic and ginger. Immediately add the soy sauce, water, brown sugar and pepper flakes. Cook the sauce for about 2 minutes and transfer to a bowl. Don't worry if the sauce doesn't look thick enough at this point. The corn starch in the beef will thicken it up later.

3. Cook the meat and assemble dish:

Turn the heat up and add the remaining oil to the wok. Add the beef and cook, stirring until it is all browned (this is a quick thing). Pour the sauce back into the wok and let it cook along with the meat. Now you can choose to cook it down and reduce the sauce or leave it thinner. Add the green onions on the last minute so the green parts will stay green and the white parts crunchy.

Serve it hot with rice.

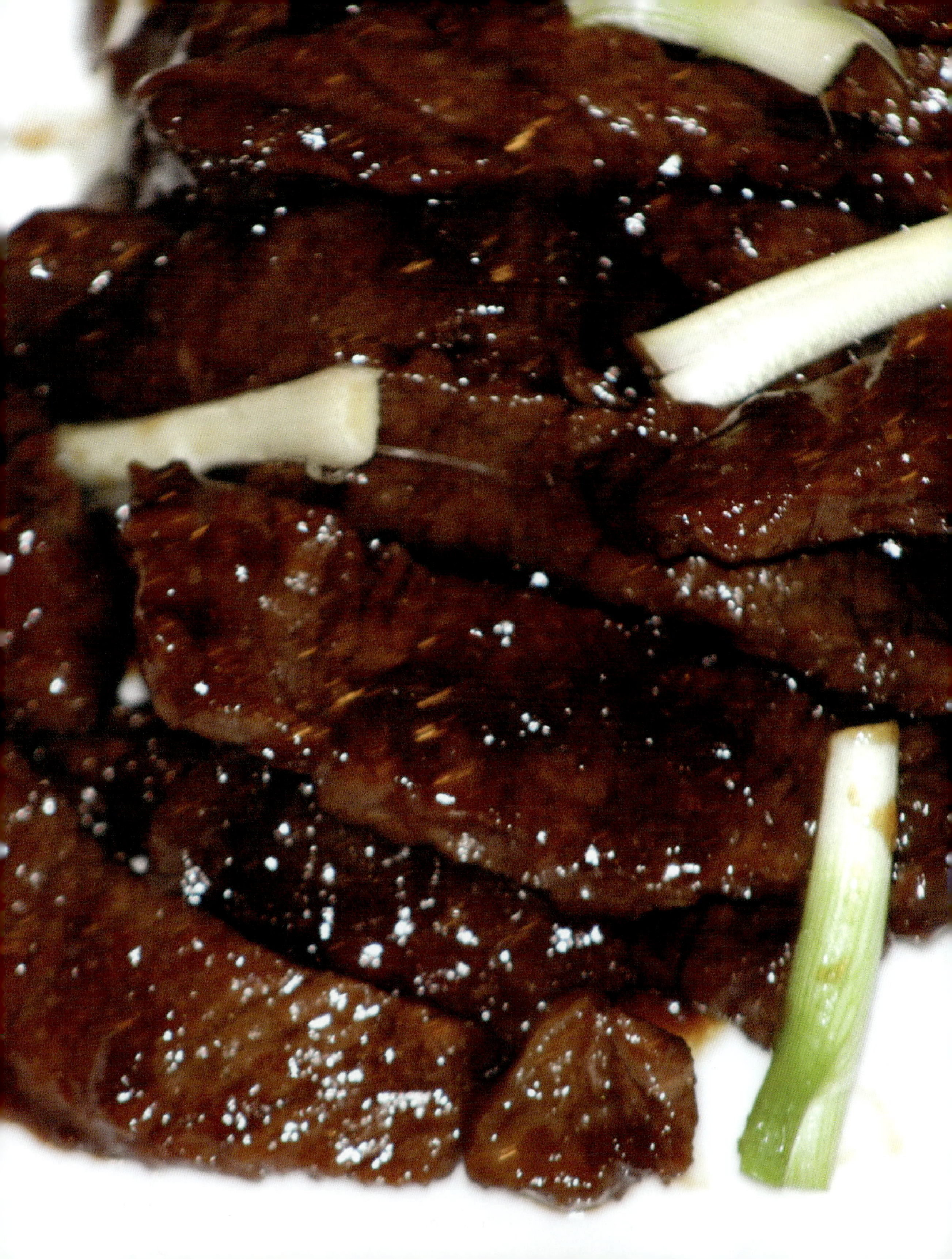

Smoked Brisket

Ingredients
- 4-5 lb. Brisket
- 2 Tbsp. meat tenderizer
- 2 oz. liquid smoke,
- 1 Tbsp. celery salt
- 1 Tbsp. paprika
- 1 tsp. onion salt
- 1/4 Tbsp. nutmeg
- 1/4 Tbsp. garlic powder,
- 1 Tbsp. brown sugar

Instructions
1. Place brisket in 9"x 13" lined with tin foil.
2. Cover w/ liquid smoke and sprinkle with tenderizer.
3. Wrap tightly in foil and refrigerate overnight
4. Next day mix remaining ingredients and sprinkle over brisket
5. Wrap tightly and bake at 300º for 2 hours
6. Loosen foil a little and bake at 200º for 5 hours.

This recipe is from Sharon Zimmerman, from Sterling, Alaska. Her husband is Dan, who refused to make a septic system out of Matt's old van (thankfully-but I wouldn't have missed the van).

Zucchini Boats

Ingredients
- 3 or 4 medium zucchini
- 1 1/2 lbs. hamburger
- 1 onion
- 1 green pepper
- 2 pieces white bread
- 8 oz. mozzarella cheese
- 1 can tomato sauce (or as much as needed)

Alaska is the widest and largest state in the US. If placed over a map of the continental US, Alaska would extend from coast to coast. If Alaska was cut in half, Texas would be the 3rd largest state.

Directions
1. Peel zucchini, par boil about 10 minutes. Cool, and cut length wise.
2. Scrape out seeds.
3. Brown hamburger with onion and soak bread in milk.
4. Squeeze out bread and crumble into hamburger mixture.
5. Add tomato sauce and cheese.
6. Put mixture into boats, and bake at 350º for 20-30 minutes.

Krunch Wrap Deluxe

Ingredients

- 1 lb. ground beef or ground moose
- 1 packet taco seasoning mix
- 1 can nacho cheese
- 6 burrito-size flour tortillas
- 6 tostada shells or corn tortillas
- 1 cup sour cream
- 2 cups shredded lettuce
- 1 tomato, diced
- 1 cup shredded Mexican cheese blend

Directions

1. Cook the ground beef according to the taco seasoning packet (usually adding water)
2. Place a large tortilla down and layer it with the following:
   - Nacho cheese (it's best to warm it up first)
   - Ground beef (cooked in taco seasoning first)
   - Tostada (hard flat taco shell)
   - Shredded Cheese
   - Sour cream
   - Shredded lettuce
   - Diced tomatoes
3. Fold and wrap the tortilla around the ingredients
4. Prepare a pan with non-stick spray and cook each side on medium heat until golden brown (starting with the seam side down first).

Marlene's Favorite

Latin Tortillas

Ingredients

- Approximately 5 potatoes, diced small
- 2 handful baby carrots
- 1 lb. fried hamburger (moose or beef)
- 1 onion
- 5 garlic cloves
- 1/2 tsp. salt
- 3 Tbsp. chives
- 1/2 tsp. basil
- 3 Tbsp. parsley

Directions

1. Fry hamburger, garlic and onions together.
2. Heat baby carrots and potatoes together until soft, then drain.
3. Mix all ingredients together.
4. Wrap in Tortillas, service with sour cream and salsa on the side.

Potato Haystack Casserole

Ingredients
- 4-5 lbs. cooked shredded potatoes
- 1 cup milk
- 1 cup sour cream
- 1 pack ranch dressing mix
- 2 lbs. hamburger
- 1 package taco seasoning
- 1 tsp. salt
- 1/2 tsp pepper
- 1 small onion
- Your favorite cheese sauce
- crushed nacho chips

Directions
1. Layer potatoes in a greased 9"x13" pan.
2. Mix milk, sour cream, and ranch dressing mix together till combined.
3. Spread on top of shredded potatoes.
4. Fry hamburger with taco seasoning, salt, pepper, and onion.
5. Layer on top of ranch mixture.
6. Bake at 350º for 30 minutes.
7. Add cheese sauce and bake 10 minutes longer.
8. Before serving add crushed Nacho chips.
9. Serve with lettuce, tomatoes, and ranch dressing or sour cream.

Meatball Sub Casserole

Ingredients
- 1/3 cup chopped onion
- 1/4 cup seasoned bread crumbs
- 3 Tbsp. Parmesan cheese
- 1 lb. ground beef (or moose)
- 3/4 loaf Italian bread, cubed
- 1 (8 oz.) pkg. cream cheese, softened
- 1/2 cup mayonnaise
- 1 Tbsp. Italian season
- 2 cup shredded mozzarella cheese, divided
- 1 (28 oz.) can spaghetti sauce
- 1 cup water

Directions
1. Combine onions, bread crumbs and parmesan cheese. Mix in beef and shape into 1" balls.
2. Bake at 400° for 15-20 minutes. Arrange bread in layers in an ungreased 13"x9" pan.
3. Combine cream cheese, mayonnaise and Italian seasoning and spread over bread.
4. Sprinkle with 1/2 cup cheese. Combine sauce and water. Add meatballs and pour over cream cheese mixture.
5. Sprinkle with remaining cheese.
6. Bake uncovered at 350° for 30 minutes.

Enchilada Tator Tot Casserole

Ingredients

- 1 lb. ground beef
- 1 medium yellow onion, finely chopped
- 2 cloves garlic, minced
- 2 Tbsp. fajita seasoning (or homemade taco seasoning)
- 4 cups frozen tater tots (about 1/2 bag)
- 1 (10 oz.) can mild red enchilada sauce
- 2 cups pepper jack cheese, shredded
- 1 (2.25 oz.) can sliced black olives (optional)
- sliced green onions, diced tomatoes and sour cream, for topping

Directions

1. Preheat oven to 350º.
2. In a large skillet, over medium heat, brown ground beef along with onion and garlic.
3. Once browned, drain excess grease then return meat to skillet.
4. Next, sprinkle two tablespoons fajita seasoning onto beef. Stir well (keep skillet on a medium-low heat)
5. Then pour in enchilada sauce. Stir well.
6. Add frozen tater tots.
7. Gently stir until the tater tots are coated with sauce.
8. Turn off heat. Transfer mixture into a 9"x13" (ungreased) baking dish. Make sure it is evenly spread out.
9. Sprinkle cheese all over tater tot mixture. Top with sliced black olives.
10. Bake uncovered for 15-20 minutes.
11. Cheese should be melted and tater tots should be golden brown.
12. Serve with diced green onions, chopped tomatoes and a dollop of sour cream!

Kodiak Casserole

Ingredients

- 2 pounds ground beef
- 4 cups diced onions
- 2 garlic cloves, minced
- 3 medium green peppers, diced
- 4 cups diced celery
- 1 jar (5-3/4 oz.) stuffed green or black olives, undrained
- 1 can (4 oz.) mushroom stems and pieces, undrained
- 1 can (10-3/4 oz.) condensed tomato soup, undiluted
- 1 jar (8 oz.) picante sauce
- 1 bottle (18 ounces) barbecue sauce
- 2 Tbsp. Worcestershire sauce
- 3 to 4 cups medium egg noodles, cooked and drained
- 1 cup (4 oz.) shredded cheddar cheese

Kodiak Island is 3,588 square miles and slightly larger than Puerto Rico.

Directions

1. In a frying pan brown ground beef with onions and garlic; drain.
2. Add remaining ingredients except cheese; mix well.
3. Cover and bake at 350º for 1 hour or until hot and bubbly.
4. Sprinkle with the cheese just before serving.

Honey BBQ Boneless Chicken

Ingredients

- 2 lb. chicken tenders or boneless skinless chicken breasts, cut into strips
- 1 tsp. salt
- 1 tsp. pepper
- vegetable oil for frying
- 4 cups buttermilk, divided
- 1 Tbsp. hot sauce
- 2 cups flour
- 1 tsp. salt
- 1 tsp. pepper
- 1 tsp. garlic powder
- 1 tsp. paprika
- 1 cup barbecue sauce
- 1/4 cup honey
- 1 Tbsp. apple cider vinegar (optional)

Directions

1. Season chicken strips with salt and pepper and marinate in 2 cups buttermilk for at least 2 hours.
2. Bring oil to 350-360° in a large frying pan, about 1 inch deep.
3. Preheat oven to 350°.
4. Combine flour, salt, pepper, garlic powder and paprika in a shallow bowl and stir to combine.
5. In a separate bowl, combine 2 cups of buttermilk and hot sauce, set aside.
6. Combine barbecue sauce, honey, and apple cider vinegar in a shallow bowl, set aside.
7. Remove the chicken strips from the buttermilk and shake off the excess.
8. Dip the chicken strip in flour mixture, then in the buttermilk and hot sauce mixture, and then back in the flour mixture Shake off excess flour.
9. Gently place in the hot oil and fry, turning over when golden brown. Drain on paper towels or on a rack.
10. Repeat until all chicken has been fried. The chicken doesn't need to be cooked through because we'll be finishing it off in the oven.
11. Gently dip the strips in the barbecue sauce and honey mixture or brush the mixture onto the strips. Shake off excess.
12. Place chicken strips on a parchment lined baking sheet and bake for 20 minutes or until cooked through. Baking time will depend on the size of your chicken strips.

Note: if you want to spice these up a bit, add some hot sauce or sriracha to the honey BBQ glaze.

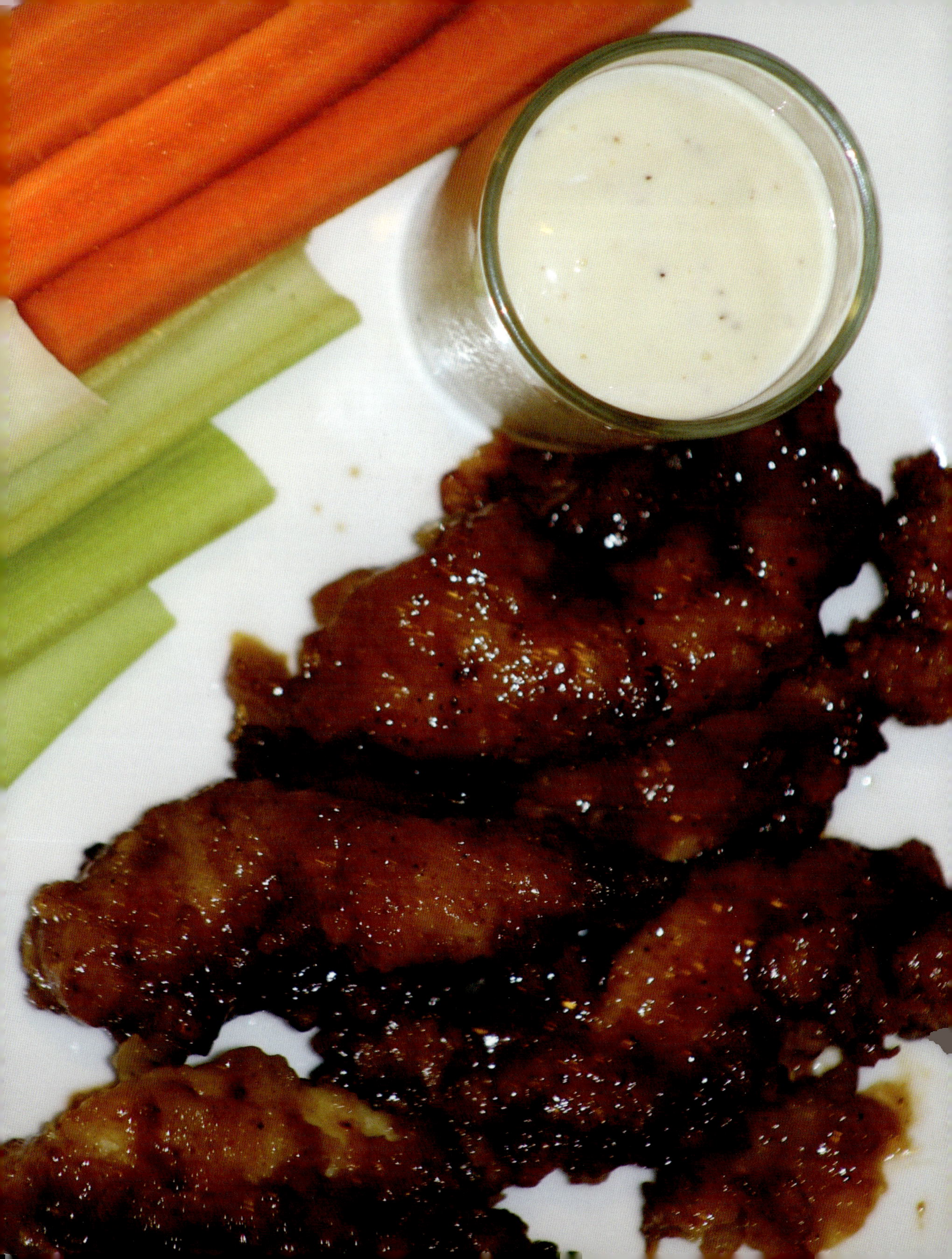

Loaded Potato Casserole

Ingredients

- 3 - 4 medium russet potatoes, scrubbed and diced (about 1.5 lbs. or 4 1/2 cups)
- 1 lb. boneless, skinless chicken breasts, diced
- 4 slices bacon, cooked crisp, cooled and crumbled
- 1 1/2 cups shredded cheddar cheese
- 4 green onions, sliced
- 1/2 tsp. salt
- 1/2 tsp. ground black pepper
- 1/2 cup heavy cream
- 2 tsp. butter, cut into small pieces

Desiree's Favorite

Directions

1. Heat oven to 350°. Lightly grease a 9" x 9" baking pan or casserole dish.
2. Spread half of the diced potatoes in bottom of pan. Place the diced chicken breasts evenly on top. Season chicken with 1/4 teaspoon each salt and pepper. Sprinkle with half the bacon crumbles, 1/2 cup of the cheese, and half the green onions.
3. Spread the remaining diced potatoes on top, followed by the remaining bacon, another 1/2 cup cheese, remaining green onions and another 1/4 teaspoon each salt and pepper. Pour heavy cream over top of casserole and then dot with the butter.
4. Cover with aluminum foil and bake in the preheated oven for 1 hour. Uncover and bake another 30 minutes.
5. In the last few minutes of baking, sprinkle with the remaining 1/2 cup cheddar cheese and bake until melted.

Campfire Chicken

Shane's Favorite

Ingredients
- Bacon
- Skinless, boneless chicken

Directions
1. Cut chicken into strips the size of your finger
2. Wrap the chicken pieces in bacon
3. Grill until bacon is crisp, check chicken, but it should also be done by then

This is one of the recipes that is so simple we almost feel bad putting it in the book and calling it a recipe. However, this delicious food never occurred to us until some friends (Tom and Anna Stauffer) told us about it. Since then we have used it many times, with many rave reviews from guests.

For an added twist, you can also smoke the bacon and chicken combination before grilling it. This gives it a pleasant smoke flavor. Of course, for optimal taste, we recommend grilling it on a wood fire in the wilderness of Alaska.

Good Chicken

Ingredients
- 4 chicken breast
- American cheese slices
- can of cream of mushroom
- 1/3 cup cooking wine
- 1/4 cup butter

Directions
1. Cover chicken breasts with American cheese.
2. Mix 1/3 cup of cooking wine with mushroom soup.
3. Spread on top of the American cheese.
4. Top with herb seasoned crouton.
5. Drizzle with 1/4 cup butter.
6. Cover and bake at 275º for 2 hours.

A dull name, but a very accurate description of this recipe!

Italian Rice Casserole

Ingredients
- 1 Tbsp. butter
- 2 cup rice
- 1 medium onion chopped
- 1 green pepper chopped
- 4 cup water
- 1/4 cup. Italian dressing
- 1 15oz. can red kidney beans
- 1 26 oz. cream of mushroom
- 6-8 slices of Velveeta
- 4 cup cooked chopped chicken or ham
- season with salt and pepper to taste

Directions
1. Lightly sauté rice, onion, pepper in butter.
2. Add water and Italian dressing. stir and bring to boil. turn off burner and cover with lid, do not lift lid for 30 min.
3. Mix beans, mushroom soup and cheese.
4. Layer in greased dish with meat of you choice. top with cheese.
5. Warm in oven.

Casserole is shown below with Dorito Salad

Hawaiian Chicken Kabobs

Ingredients
- 1/3 cup ketchup
- 1/3 cup packed dark brown sugar
- 1/3 cup low-sodium soy sauce
- 1/4 cup pineapple juice
- 4 Tbsp. olive oil, divided, plus more for brushing grill
- 1 1/2 Tbsp. rice vinegar
- 4 garlic cloves, minced (4 tsp)
- 1 Tbsp. minced ginger
- 1/2 tsp. sesame oil
- Salt and freshly ground black pepper
- 1 3/4 lb boneless, skinless chicken breast, chopped into 1 1/4-inch cubes
- 3 cups (heaping) fresh cubed pineapple (about 3/4 of 3 lb. pineapple)
- 1 1/2 large green peppers, diced into 1 1/4-inch pieces
- 1 large red onion, diced into 1 1/4-inch pieces

Matt's Favorite

Directions
1. In a mixing bowl whisk together ketchup, brown sugar, soy sauce, pineapple juice, 2 Tbsp. olive oil, rice vinegar, garlic, ginger and sesame oil.
2. Stir in 3/4 tsp pepper and season with salt if desired.
3. Place chicken in a gallon size resalable bag.
4. Reserve 1/2 cup of the marinade in refrigerator then pour remaining marinade over chicken.
5. Seal bag and refrigerate 3 hours (meanwhile soak 10 wooden skewer sticks in water for 1 hour).
6. Preheat a grill over medium heat to 400 degrees. Meanwhile, drizzle remaining 2 Tbsp. olive oil over red onion, bell pepper and pineapple and toss.
7. Season red onion and bell pepper with salt and pepper, then thread red onion, bell pepper, pineapple and chicken onto skewers until all of the chicken has been used.
8. Brush grill grates with olive oil then place skewers on grill.
9. Grill 5 minutes then brush along tops with 1/4 cup of remaining marinade.
10. Rotate to opposite side and brush remaining 1/4 cup of marinade on opposite side and allow to grill about 4 minutes longer, or until chicken registers 165 degrees in center on an instant read thermometer.
11. Serve warm.

This recipe is Matt's favorite! They work great on the grill or over a campfire, and are very easy to make.

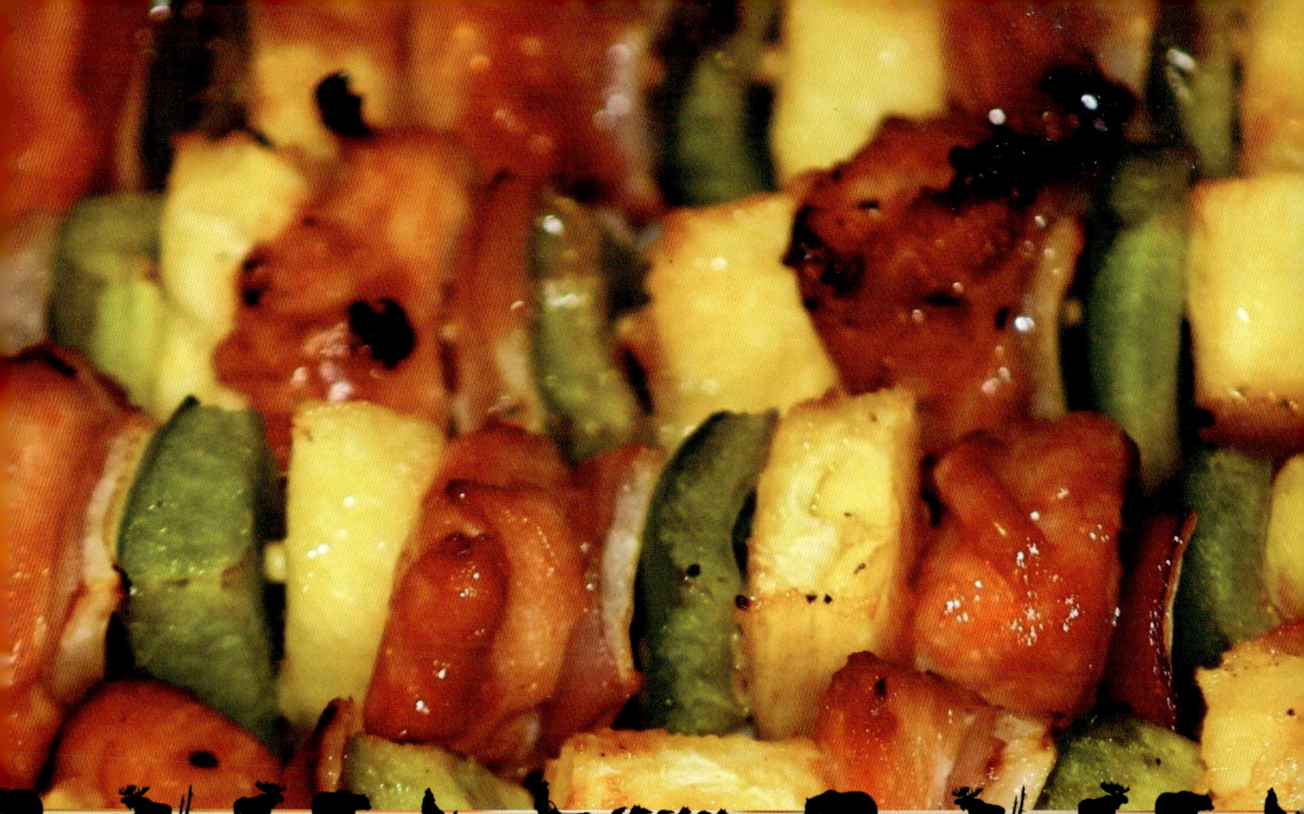

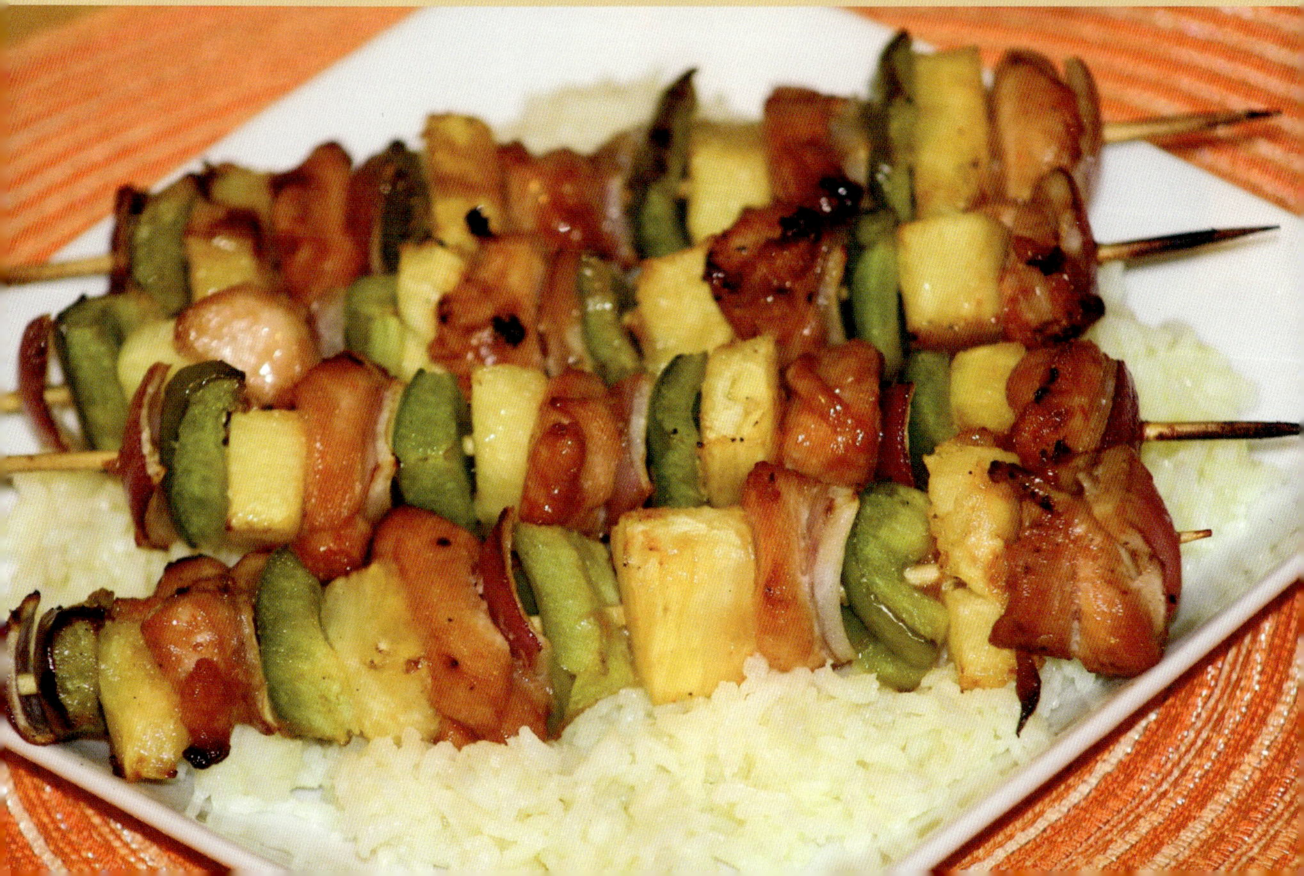

Crockpot Creamy Italian Chicken

Ingredients

- 4 boneless, skinless chicken breast halves
- 1 envelope Italian salad dressing mix
- 1/4 cup water
- 8 oz. Cream cheese, softened
- 1 can cream of chicken soup
- 4 oz. Mushroom stems and pieces (drained)
- Hot cooked noodles or rice

Directions

1. Place chicken in a slow cooker.
2. Combine salad dressing mix and water. Pour over chicken.
3. Cover and cook on low for three hours.
4. In a small bowl, beat cream cheese and soup until combined.
5. Stir in mushrooms and pour over chicken.
6. Cook one hour longer, or until chicken juices run clear.
7. Serve over rice or noodles.

Baked Ziti with Parmesan Topping

Ingredients

- 1 lb. ziti pasta, cooked and drained
- 2 cups (15 oz.) Part-Skim Ricotta Cheese
- 2 cups (8 oz.) Shredded Mozzarella Cheese
- 1 egg, beaten
- 1/2 tsp. pepper
- 1 jar (24 oz.) Tomato Sauce, divided
- 1/4 cup (1 oz.) Shredded Parmesan Cheese

Directions

1. Combine ziti, Ricotta cheese, Mozzarella cheese, egg, pepper and 1-1/2 cups pasta sauce in large bowl.
2. Spread pasta mixture in 13"x9" inch baking dish; top with remaining sauce. Sprinkle with Parmesan cheese.
3. Bake uncovered in preheated 375° oven 40 minutes or until heated through. Let stand 10 minutes before serving.

Poor Man's Lobster (Halibut)

Ingredients
- cup sugar
- halibut, cut in about 1 inch cubes, or use cheeks
- butter, for dipping (not margarine)

Directions
1. Fill a pot with water (about a gallon).
2. Add 1 cup sugar, and bring to a boil.
3. Do not ever stir the mixture.
4. Add chunks of halibut, do not over crowd.
5. They will sink to the bottom, and then rise to the top when they are done.
6. It should take just a few minutes.
7. Remove with slotted spoon.
8. Remember to not stir the mixture.
9. Continue until all the halibut is cooked.
10. Dip in melted butter and eat!

Our own tartar sauce
- 3 Tbsp. relish
- 1-2 Tbsp. mustard
- 1 cup mayo

The irony in this recipe is that if you buy Halibut, it usually costs more per pound than Lobster.

Brown Sugar Rub Salmon

Ingredients
1 cup firmly packed light brown sugar
1/2 cup paprika
1/4 cup kosher salt
2 Tbsp. dried thyme
1 (2-pound) salmon fillet, cut into portions

Directions
1. Combine first 4 ingredients.
2. Rub spice mixture over top of salmon; let stand 10 minutes.
3. Grill salmon over medium-high heat 3 to 4 minutes on each side or until desired degree of doneness, or can also be broiled for several minutes.

Heavenly Halibut

Ingredients
- 1/2 cup parmesan cheese, grated
- 1/4 cup butter, softened
- 3 Tbsp. mayonnaise
- 2 Tbsp. lemon juice
- 3 Tbsp. green onions, chopped
- 1/4 tsp. salt
- 1 dash hot pepper sauce
- 2 lbs. halibut, fillets, skinless

The Alaska state record for a Halibut is 482 pounds!

Directions:
1. Preheat the oven broiler and grease a baking dish.
2. In a bowl, mix the parmesan cheese, butter, mayonnaise, lemon juice, green onions, salt, and hot pepper sauce.
3. Arrange the halibut fillets in the prepared baking dish.
4. Broil halibut filets 8 minutes in the prepared oven, or until easily flaked with a fork. Spread the parmesan cheese mixture on top of filets, and continue broiling 2 minutes, or until topping is bubbly and lightly browned.

Tuna Twirls

Ingredients

- 3 Tbsp. butter
- 2 Tbsp. chopped onion
- 1/2 tsp. salt
- 1 1/2 cup milk
- 6 Tbsp. flour
- 1 can cream of chicken soup
- 1 can tuna
- 1/2 cup grated cheese
- 2 cups Bisquick
- 1/2 cup water

Directions

1. Melt butter, add onion, salt, flour, milk, chicken soup and tuna.
2. Cook until thickened.
3. Pour into casserole dish and top with biscuits.
4. To make biscuits mix Bisquick and water, roll out to 1/4".
5. Sprinkle cheese over dough; roll up and slice 1/2".
6. Put on top of sauce and bake at 450° for 15 minutes.

Rachel Casserole

Ingredients
- 1 lb. sliced turkey, coarsely chopped
- 16 ounces sauerkraut, drained and rinsed
- 1 cup Thousand Island salad dressing
- 2 1/2 cups shredded Swiss cheese
- 6 slices Rye bread, cubed

Instructions
1. Preheat oven to 400º.
2. Layer turkey on the bottom of a 9"x13" baking dish.
3. Make sure the sauerkraut is drained and patted dry. Sprinkle it on top of the turkey.
4. Drizzle the dressing on top of the sauerkraut and sprinkle the Swiss cheese on top.
5. Arrange the diced bread on top of the casserole and lightly spray it with cooking spray so that it toasts up nicely (or you can butter the bread).
6. Bake for 20-25 minutes or until bread is toasted and cheese has melted.

Crab Au Gratin

Ingredients
- 2 1/2 lbs. crab meat
- 2 Tbsp. butter
- 1 cup heavy cream
- 1 cup shredded cheddar cheese
- 2 Tbsp. Parsley
- Crushed ritz crackers

Directions
1. Mix all ingredients except ritz crackers.
2. Bake at 350° until warmed.
3. Sprinkle with crushed ritz crackers before serving.

Chicken Bacon Ranch Casserole

Ingredients

- 4 slices bacon, diced
- 2 boneless, skinless chicken thighs cut into 1-inch chunks
- 1 Tbsp. olive oil
- 4 Tbsp. Ranch Seasoning and Salad Dressing Mix, or more, to taste
- 8 ounces rotini
- 1 cup shredded mozzarella cheese
- 1/2 cup shredded cheddar cheese
- 2 Tbsp. chopped fresh parsley leaves
- For the alfredo sauce
- 2 Tbsp. unsalted butter
- 3 cloves garlic, minced
- 1 cup heavy cream, or more, to taste
- 1/4 cup freshly grated Parmesan
- Kosher salt and freshly ground black pepper, to taste

Directions

1. Preheat oven to 375°. Lightly oil a 9"×9" baking dish or coat with nonstick spray.
2. To make the alfredo sauce, melt butter in a saucepan over medium heat. Add garlic, and cook, stirring frequently, about 1-2 minutes. Gradually whisk in heavy cream. Cook, whisking constantly, until incorporated, about 1-2 minutes. Stir in Parmesan until slightly thickened, about 1-2 minutes. If the mixture is too thick, add more heavy cream as needed; season with salt and pepper, to taste. Set aside.
3. Fry bacon. Drain excess fat; reserving 1 Tbsp. in the skillet. Transfer bacon to a paper towel-lined plate.
4. In a gallon size Ziploc bag, add chicken, 1 Tbsp. olive oil and Ranch Seasoning, shaking to coat thoroughly.
5. Add chicken to the skillet and cook, flipping once, until cooked through, about 2-3 minutes on each side; set aside.
6. In a large pot of boiling salted water, cook pasta according to package instructions; drain well.
7. Add pasta to the prepared baking dish and layer with chicken and alfredo sauce; sprinkle with cheeses and bacon. Place into oven and bake until bubbly and heated through, about 15-20 minutes.
8. Serve immediately, garnished with parsley, if desired.

Alaska has many kinds of wild berries that are great to eat! They are usually ready in August. The downside? If you eat the wrong berry, you could go into cardiac arrest. Always make sure to take a good berry guide book along!

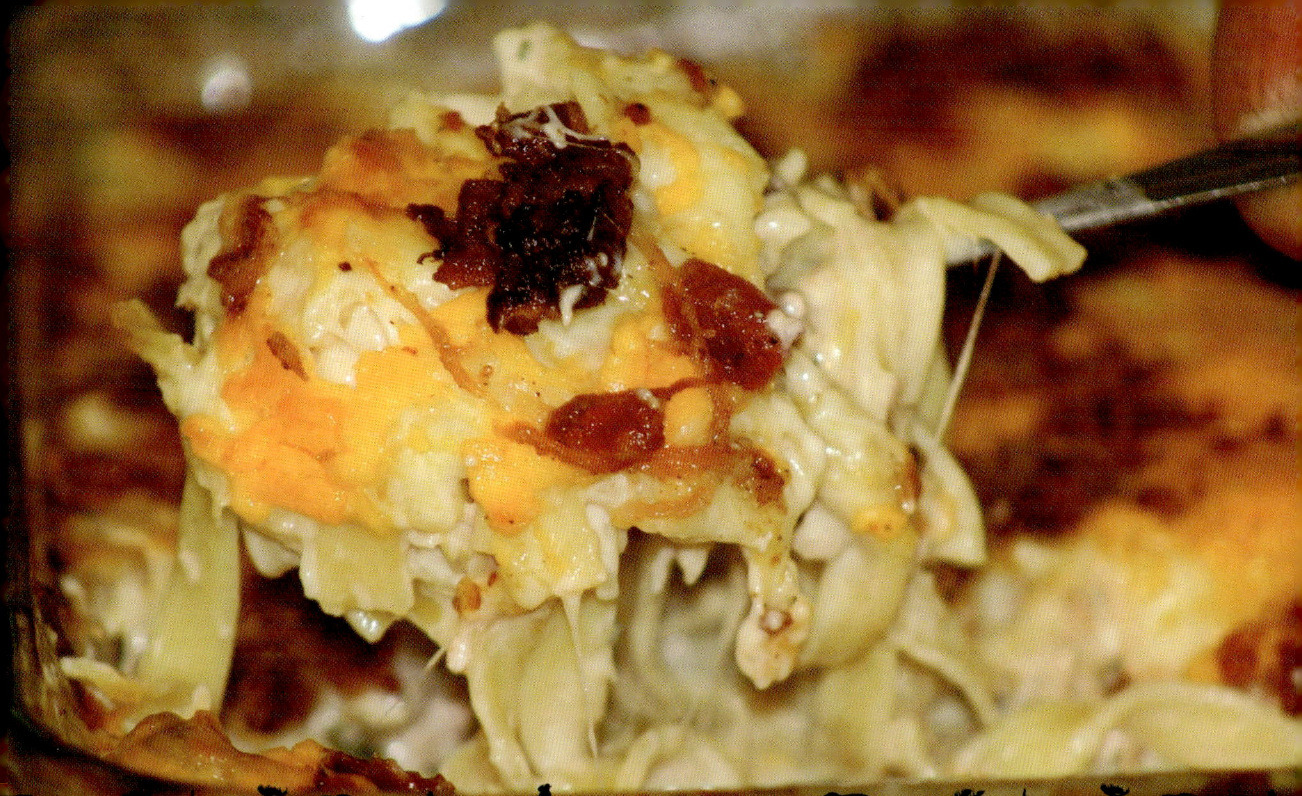

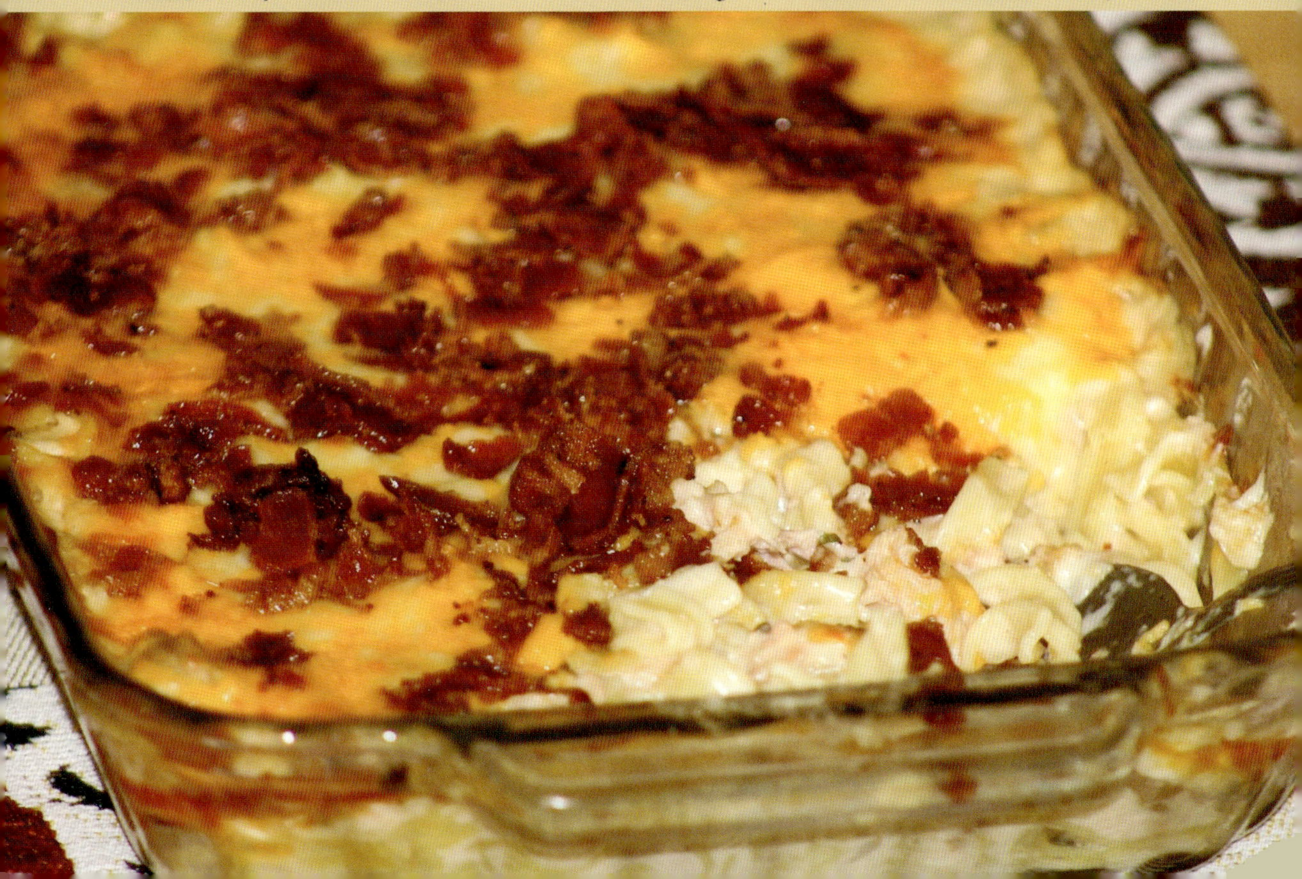

BLT Pizza

Ingredients

- 1 Tbsp. dry yeast
- 1/4 cup warm water
- 1 tsp. salt
- 1 tsp. honey or brown sugar
- 2 Tbsp. vegetable oil
- 3/4 cup cool water
- 3 cups flour

Directions

1. Dissolve yeast in warm water, let proof 10 min.
2. Meanwhile, combine salt, honey, veg. oil, and cool water.
3. Mix well, then add flour and yeast mixture.
4. Sprinkle 1-2 cups of cheese on the crust before baking.
5. Bake at 400º, till done.
6. Cool the pizza crust 5 minutes.
7. Spread mayo on to your satisfaction.
8. Chop about a head of lettuce.
9. Chop approx. 2 tomatoes.
10. Crumble one pack of fried bacon on top.

Samantha's Favorite

BLT Pizza is a family favorite. We first discovered BLT pizza at a pizza shop, but it was too far away to frequent, so we ended up developing our own recipe. It's also cheaper to make yourself.

Wolves in Alaska can exceed 150 pounds, although most are smaller.

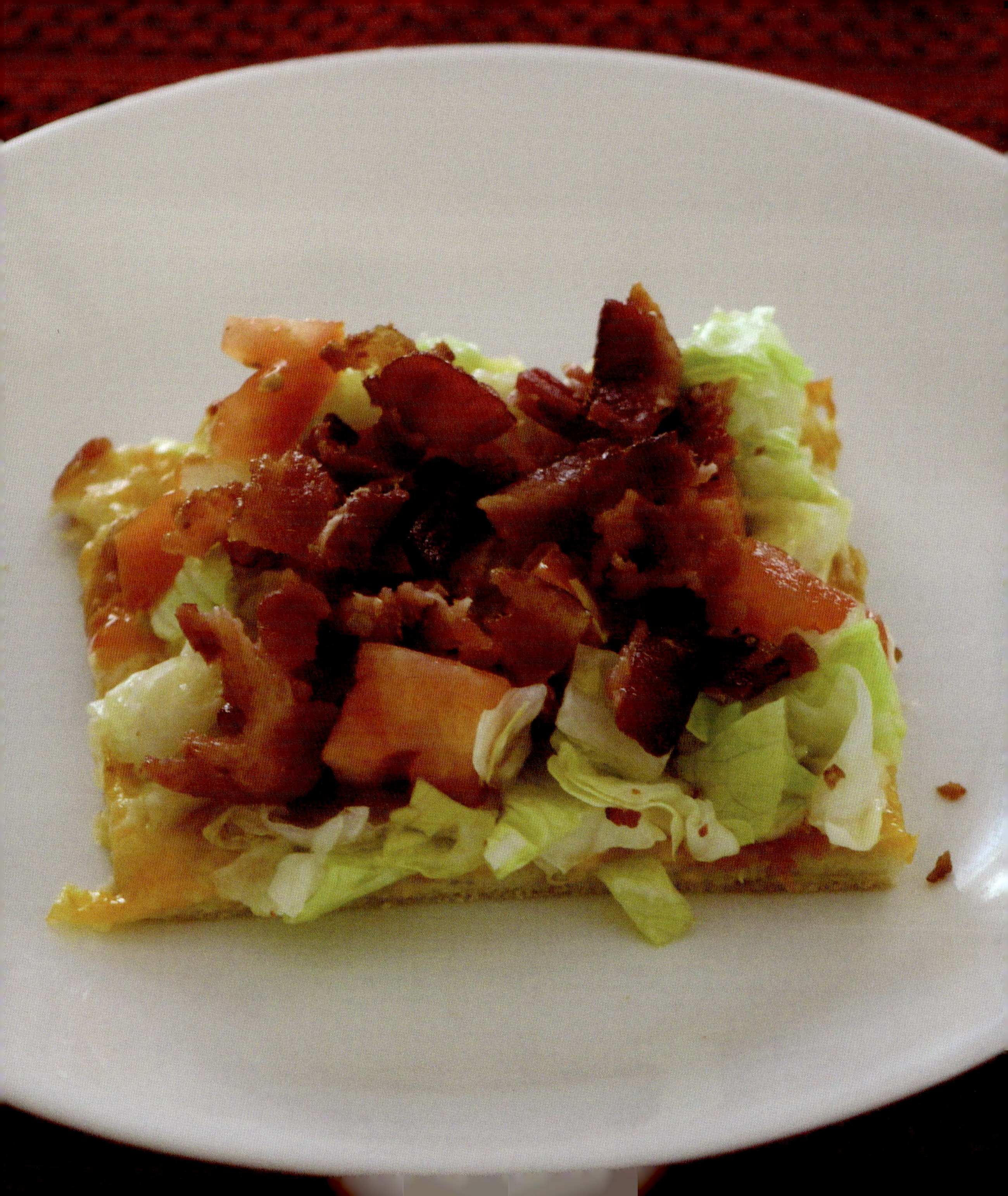

Our 40 Acres and Cabin

While building our cabin and camping out on our land, we often enjoyed campfire chicken, along with Ramen noodles and baked beans (sorry, we didn't include those recipes). For the most part, I enjoyed camping. The weather was very nice and unseasonably warm during the day. But overnight it would get so cold my bones hurt. I could feel the cold seeping up through the ground, and into our air mattress. Matt was more scared of bears that I was, but that was because I knew he would just scare them off with his big gun. Bears turned out to be a non issue, and we have never seen any at our cabin.

Buying the land was exciting, and I didn't object to Matt doing this. The thought of building a cabin sounded like a lot of fun. However, Matt's expectations for building were terribly unrealistic. He thought we could have the cabin up in a week, but it took several weeks.

While building, we cooked most of our food over the campfire and our little propane cook stove. I washed the dishes in bowls I brought along. Sometimes we would get subs and pizza, but the food would be cold by the time we got back from town.

It seemed like the children were always dirty, but they thrived in it. Shane quickly learned how to drive the four wheeler. Samantha was at the age where she would get into everything, so the older children took turns playing toys with her in the tent. This resulted in lots of sand being drug into the tent, which we ended up sleeping on at night. This was not as relaxing as what I imagine sleeping on the beach would be…

Eventually the cabin got built, and then all the dirt followed us in there. With no front porch, the floor was always dirty. Later we added the front porch, which made it much easier to keep the cabin floor clean.

We bought all our furniture and many cabin supplies on craigslist, except our bunk bed cots. One time Matt bought some big water barrels for the cabin, but somewhere along the way home they flew off the trailer. We never did find them. Later we found some cheap barrels at a yard sale. The craigslist and yard sale deals saved us a lot of money furnishing the cabin.

Above: Ariel photo of our cabin and land. Below: Matt and Shane work on making a campfire to grill some chicken, in Marlin Eicher's fire ring he loaned us, during cabin construction.

Above: The tent we stayed in, which Marlin loaned us. Below: I am holding Samantha beside the cabin construction site. Behind me are Desiree and Lana.

Above: The girls playing in the tent with Samantha. Below: Always dirt everywhere! But at least the children were happy!

Side Dishes

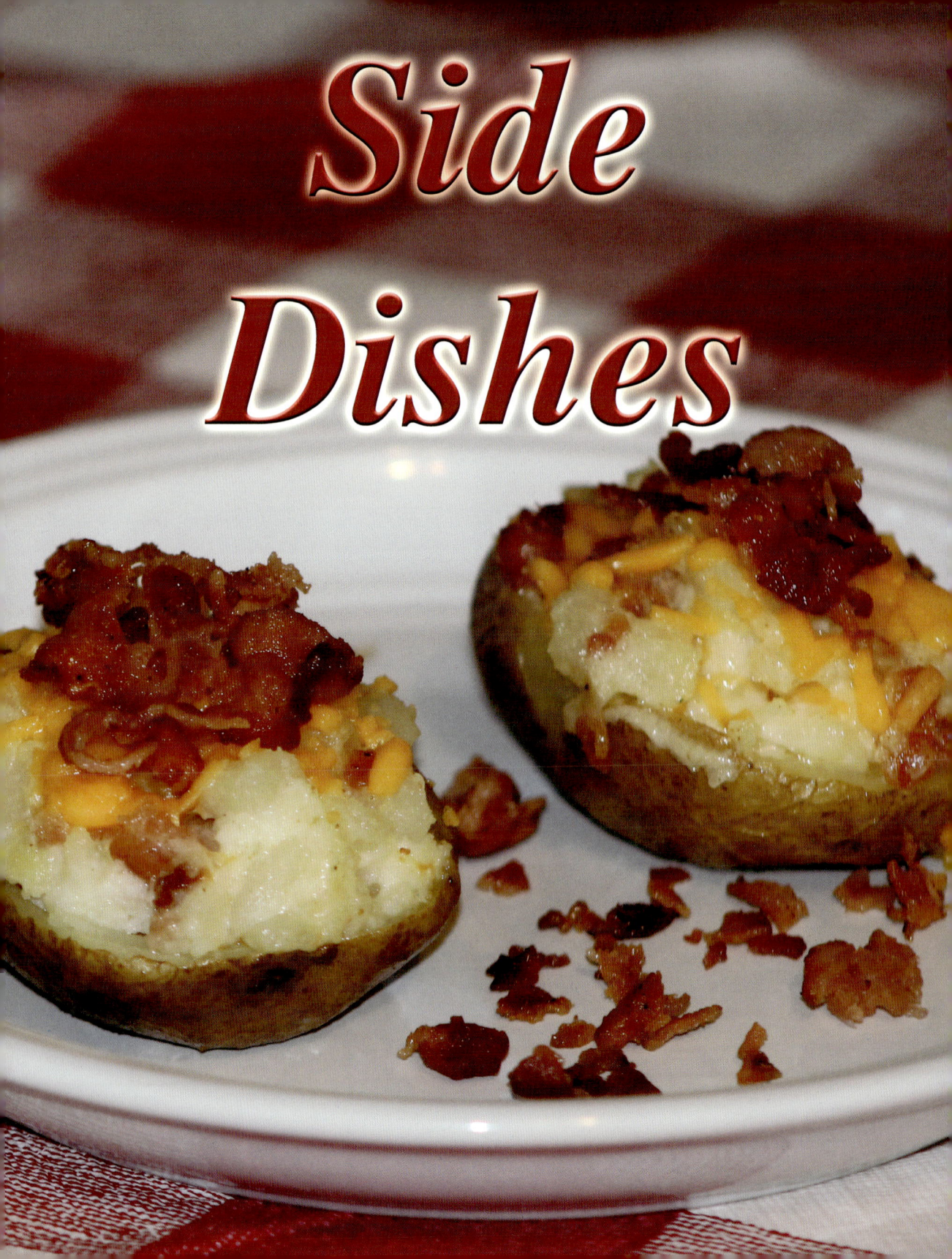

Roasted Parmesan Sweet Potatoes

Ingredients
- 2 sweet potatoes (peeled and cubed)
- 2 tsp. minced garlic
- 1 Tbsp. olive oil
- 2 Tbsp. butter (melted)
- 4 Tbsp. grated Parmesan Cheese
- 1/2 tsp. garlic salt
- 1/2 tsp. Italian Seasoning
- dried parsley

Alaska has coastlines on three different seas: Arctic Ocean, Pacific Ocean, and Bering Sea.

Directions
1. Preheat oven to 400º.
2. Peel and cube sweet potatoes into 1 inch cubes.
3. Place garlic, oil, butter, salt, Parmesan cheese and Italian seasoning in a ziploc bag and mix well.
4. Throw in sweet potatoes and shake until well coated.
5. Place aluminum foil on cookie sheet and lightly spray.
6. Place coated sweet potatoes onto cookie sheet and spread out evenly.
7. Bake for 18-22 minutes.
8. Serve warm and sprinkle with dried parsley if desired.

Canadian Poutine

Ingredients
- French Fries
- Brown gravy
- Cheese curds or tiny blocks of your favorite white cheese.

If you drive directly to Alaska from Pennsylvania, you will spend more time driving in Canada than the United States.

Directions
1. Make fries however you wish. (We are assuming you know how to make French fries)
2. Cover with your favorite brown gravy.
3. Add cheese. Cheese curds taste the best, however cheese blocks will also work.

This recipe is very simple, so simple in fact you may be insulted that we put it in a cookbook. However, this simple culinary delight never occurred to us until we drove through Canada the first time. Now on every trip through Canada we stop for poutine, which is served at almost every restaurant, including the big fast food chains.

Kallia's Favorite

Cheesy Potatoes

Ingredients
- 6 medium potatoes peeled cooked and mashed
- 1-8oz. french onion dip
- 1 cup cottage cheese
- salt and pepper to taste
- 1/2 cup cheddar cheese

Directions
1. Mix and sprinkle with cheddar cheese.
2. Put in greased dish.
3. Bake 350º for 30-40 minutes.

On March 7, 1964 a 9.2 magnitude earthquake struck Alaska, causing over $311 million dollars in damage. This is known as the "Great Alaskan Earthquake" or the "Good Friday Earthquake."

Twice Baked Potatoes

Ingredients
- 8 Potatoes
- 2 sticks butter
- 1 cup Sour Cream
- 1 cup Cheddar/Jack Cheese
- 1 cup Bacon
- 1/4 tsp Lawry's Seasoned Salt
- Black Pepper
- milk (if necessary)
- 2/3 of a Green Onion (optional)

Directions
1. Wash, then place eight baking potatoes on a cookie sheet. Bake in a 400º oven for 1 hour, 15 minutes, making sure they're sufficiently cooked through.
2. Let them cool, then cut in half and scrape out the inside. Leave enough of potato skin, so it doesn't fall apart.
3. Mash potatoes with a fork. Mix one cup bacon, with butter, sour cream, and seasonings. Then add filling into hollow potato skins, and top with green onions and extra shredded cheese.
4. Bake at 350º for 15- 20 minutes.

Buttery Crusted Baked Pototoes

Ingredients
- 6 red potatoes, washed and dried
- 6 tablespoons salted butter, melted
- 1 cup crushed butter crackers (round Ritz-style crackers)
- 1/2 tsp. salt (optional)

Instructions
1. Preheat the oven to 425°. Spray a baking sheet with cooking spray.
2. Cut the washed and dried red potatoes in half.
3. Pour the melted butter in a bowl and place the crushed crackers in another bowl.
4. Dunk the potato halves first in butter, then coat them in cracker crumbs.
5. Place the potatoes cut side down on a baking sheet.
6. Bake at 425° for 30-40 minutes or until the potatoes are soft throughout.

Ultimate Scalloped Potatoes

Ingredients
- 1 tsp. butter, softened
- 1 cup heavy whipping cream
- 1/3 cup milk
- 1 tsp. salt
- 1/2 tsp. pepper
- 2 garlic cloves, crushed
- 6 medium potatoes
- 1 cup (4 ounces) shredded Swiss cheese
- 1/4 cup shredded Parmesan cheese

Directions
1. Grease a shallow 1-1/2-quart baking dish with the butter; set aside. In a large saucepan, combine the cream, milk, salt, pepper and garlic. Cook just until bubbles begin to form around sides of pan. Remove from the heat; cool for 10 minutes.
2. Peel and thinly slice the potatoes; pat dry with paper towels. Layer half of the potatoes in prepared baking dish; top with half of the cream mixture and half of the cheeses. Repeat layers.
3. Bake, uncovered, at 350° for 55-65 minutes or until potatoes are tender. Let stand for 5-10 minutes before serving. Yield: 6 servings.

Brown Sugar Red Potatoes

Ingredients

- 4-6 red potatoes (cubed)
- 1/2 cup water
- 1 1/2 Tbsp. butter
- 1 1/2 Tbsp. brown sugar
- parsley (or your favorite spice)
- garlic salt & pepper to taste

Instructions

1. Bring red potatoes, water, butter and brown sugar to a boil in a pan over medium-high heat.
2. Turn to low and simmer for approximately 6 minutes.
3. Turn back to high and cook until all the water is evaporated and potatoes s are tender. It took me another 10-15 minutes.
4. Remove from heat. Salt and Pepper, sprinkle with parsley and enjoy!

Lemon Herb Potatoes

Ingredients
- 8-10 potatoes, chopped into chunks
- Juice of 1 small lemon
- 2 Tbsp. olive oil
- 1/4 tsp. salt
- 1/4 tsp. black pepper
- 1/4 tsp. garlic powder
- 1/2 tsp. dried oregano
- 1/2 tsp. dried thyme
- 1/2 tsp. dried rosemary
- 4-5 cloves garlic, smashed

Thompson pass, near Valdez, Alaska, receives an average snowfall of 551 inches a year. Thompson pass is a 2805 foot gap in the Chugach Mountains.

Directions
1. Preheat oven to 375 degrees. Place a baking sheet or 9"x13" inch pan into the oven and bring it to temperature while the oven preheats (you want it hot).
2. Meanwhile, boil the chopped potatoes in lightly salted water for about 5, drain and toss into a large mixing bowl with the lemon juice, olive oil, salt, pepper, garlic powder, oregano, thyme, rosemary and garlic cloves.
3. Pour the coated potatoes onto the hot baking sheet or into the baking dish and bake for 1 hour, tossing every 20 minutes to get an even brown on all sides.

Brown Sugar Green Beans

Ingredients
- 1 (16 oz.) pkg. Frozen green beans
- 6 strips bacon, cooked and cut into 1" pieces
- 1/4 cup butter
- 1/4 cup light brown sugar
- garlic salt to taste

The largest gold nugget found in Alaska weighed over 20 pounds! The value of this nugget, going by September 2016 gold spot price, is over $380,000.

Directions
1. In a large skillet, fry the bacon until done but not quite crisp.
2. Drain off grease and add butter and sugar.
3. Cook, until sugar dissolved.
4. Cook beans according to your liking.
5. Drain water from beans, season with garlic salt, and stir in sugar and bacon mixture.
6. Serve immediately.

Hush Puppies

Ingredients
- 1 3/4 cups self-rising cornmeal
- 1/2 cup self-rising flour
- 1 tsp. seasoned salt
- 2 tsp. sugar
- 2 eggs, slightly beaten
- 1 cup buttermilk
- 2 Tbsp. melted bacon grease-or butter can also be used.
- 1 small onion, minced

The Trans-Alaska pipeline runs from Prudhoe Bay to Valdez, and was finished in 1977. As of 2010, the pipeline has transported 16 billion barrels of oil.

Directions
1. Heat a minimum of 4 inches of oil in a deep skillet or wide pan to 350º (medium-high heat).
2. Mix cornmeal, flour, seasoned salt and sugar in a medium bowl. In a separate bowl combine eggs, buttermilk and bacon grease or butter and mix well. Slowly add wet ingredients and minced onion to cornmeal mixture stirring by hand. Stir until just combined.
3. Using a teaspoon, drop heaping spoonfuls of batter into hot grease. Cook hush puppies until golden brown (approximately 4-5 minutes), turning once. Hush puppies will often flip over on their own when the bottom side is ready.

Rainbow Roasted Vegetables

Ingredients
- 1 2/3 cup chopped red bell peppers
- 2 cups chopped carrots
- 1 1/3 cup chopped yellow bell peppers or yellow zucchini
- 1 1/3 cup chopped zucchini
- 1 cup broccoli florets
- 1 cup chopped red onions
- 1 Tbsp. dried thyme
- Balsamic vinegar to taste

A full grown moose will drink 10-15 gallons of water a day!

Directions
1. Preheat the oven to 390 ºF
2. Place the chopped vegetables onto a baking sheet, add the thyme and balsamic vinegar to taste.
3. Bake for about 25 minutes or until the vegetables are cooked.

Honey Roasted Carrots

Ingredients

- 1 lbs. baby carrots
- 3 Tbsp. olive oil
- 3 Tbsp. honey
- salt and pepper to taste

The long summer daylight hours make Alaskan grown carrots taste much sweeter than the same variety of carrots raised in the lower 48.

Directions

1. Preheat oven to 400º.
2. Line a baking sheet with foil and spray lightly with non-stick cooking spray. In a bowl, mix together carrots and olive oil until carrots are all covered.
3. Spread the carrots in a single layer on the baking sheet. Drizzle the honey over the carrots and sprinkle salt and pepper on top.
4. Bake uncovered, turning once, under just tender (about 25-30 minutes).

Loaded Roasted Broccoli

Ingredients
- 2 cups broccoli florets
- 1 Tbsp. olive oil
- 2 cups of cauliflower
- 1 Tbsp. butter
- 1 cup of cheddar cheese, shredded
- salt & pepper to taste
- 3 pieces of bacon, cooked and crumbled
- 4 green onions chopped

The largest salmon ever caught in Alaska was a King Salmon weighing 97.5 pounds, caught in the Kenai River.

Directions
1. Preheat oven to 375°.
2. Toss broccoli with olive oil and roast in the oven for 30 minutes or until cooked and slightly browned.
3. Meanwhile add cauliflower and butter to a microwave bowl and cook in the microwave for 10 minutes or until the cauliflower can be easily pierced with a fork.
4. Let cauliflower cool a few minutes and then add to a high speed blender with the cheese.
5. Blend until smooth and creamy.
6. When broccoli is cooked, top with cheese, bacon and any other toppings you wish.

Egg Salad Divan

Ingredients
- 8 hard cooked eggs, peeled
- 1/2 cup Miracle Whip
- 1 tsp. mustard
- 1/4 tsp. salt
- 1/8 tsp. pepper
- 2 Tbsp. butter
- 2 Tbsp. flour
- 1/4 tsp. salt
- 1/8 tsp. paprika
- 1 cup milk
- 3/4 cup shredded Swiss cheese
- 2 lbs. fresh asparagus spears, cooked, drained

Alaska has over 3 million lakes and 3,000 rivers! The largest river in Alaska is the Yukon River, which is also the 3rd largest river in North America.

Directions
1. Halve eggs lengthwise. Remove yolks, mash yolks, stir in next 4 ingredients.
2. Spoon into egg white halves.
3. In 2 quart saucepan over medium heat, melt butter, stir in flour and next 3 ingredients until smooth. Stir in milk.
4. Cook, stirring constantly, until mixture boils. Stir in cheese until melted.
5. Remove from heat, spread 1/2 of sauce in bottom of 13"x9" baking dish.
6. Arrange cooked asparagus alternately with salad egg halves in diagonal rows in dish.
7. Spoon remaining sauce over asparagus. Bake at 400° in oven until hot.

Cheesy Corn

Ingredients
- 9-1/2 cups (48 oz.) frozen corn
- 11 oz. cream cheese, softened
- 1/4 cup butter, cubed
- 3 Tbsp. water
- 3 Tbsp. milk
- 2 Tbsp. sugar
- 6 slices process American cheese, cut into small pieces

Sweet corn can be grown in the interior of Alaska without a green house. However the temperatures near the coast are too cool for sweet corn to grow properly, unless planted in a greenhouse.

Directions
1. In a 4- or 5-qt. slow cooker, combine all ingredients.
2. Cook, covered, on low, until heated through and cheese is melted, 3-4 hours, stirring once. Yield: 12 servings.

Best Brussel Sprouts

Ingredients

- 1 1/2 lbs. fresh Brussels sprouts, cleaned and halved (or frozen)
- 4 Tbsp. of butter
- 2 cloves fresh garlic, minced
- 2 chicken bouillon cubes
- 3 slices of minced bacon
- pepper to taste

Directions

1. Prepare a pot of boiling water and cook the Brussels sprouts in it for about 3 minutes, if frozen cook longer.
2. Drain and set aside.
3. Cook the bacon in a large frying pan.
4. Add garlic, butter, bouillon, and cook until garlic is tender.
5. Add Brussels sprouts to the mix, and sauté for about 5 minutes over medium low heat.
6. Season with pepper and serve.

Grandma's Filling

Ingredients
- 4 quarts cubed bread
- 1 cup mashed potatoes
- 2 cups milk
- 1 cup chicken broth
- 4 eggs
- 2 tsp. turmeric
- 1 Tbsp. Season all
- 1 tsp. pepper
- 1 Tbsp. parsley
- 2 ribs celery
- 1 small onion
- 2 Tbsp. chicken base
- 1/2 cup butter

Directions
1. Mix bread and all seasonings.
2. Sauté onions and peppers in butter and chicken base.
3. Mix onions and peppers with the bread, and add the mashed potatoes.
4. Combine milk, beaten eggs, and chicken broth.
5. Mix everything, and bake at 350º for 45 minutes.
6. Stir it after it was baking 20 minutes, if it seems too dry add more chicken broth.

Zucchini Corn Pancakes

These easy pancakes are the perfect side dish or appetizer to any meal. And best of all, they don't even taste "healthy"!

Ingredients
- 1 pound zucchini, grated
- 2 teaspoon salt
- 1 cup corn kernels, frozen, canned or roasted
- 4 large eggs, beaten
- 1/2 teaspoon dried basil
- 1/2 teaspoon dried oregano
- 1/4 teaspoon garlic powder
- freshly ground black pepper, to taste
- 1/2 cup shredded cheddar cheese
- 3/4 cups all-purpose flour
- 2 tablespoons olive oil

Alaska has the highest concentration of pilots of all the US states. 1 out of every 58 Alaskans has a pilot's license, and one out of 59 owns a plane.

Instructions
1. Place grated zucchini in a colander over the sink. Add salt and gently toss to combine; let sit for 10 minutes. Using a clean dish towel or cheese cloth, drain zucchini completely.
2. In a large bowl, combine zucchini, corn, eggs, basil, oregano and garlic powder; season with salt and pepper, to taste. Stir in cheese and flour until well combined.
3. Heat olive oil in a large skillet over medium high heat. Scoop tablespoons of batter for each pancake, flattening with a spatula, and cook until the underside is nicely golden brown, about 2 minutes. Flip and cook on the other side, about 1-2 minutes longer.

Zucchini Pie

Ingredients

- 4-5 cups thinly sliced zucchini
- 1 large onion, diced
- 2 Tbsp. butter
- 2 Tbsp. dried parsley flakes
- 1/2 tsp. salt
- 1/2 tsp. pepper
- 1/2 tsp. garlic powder
- 1/2 tsp. dried oregano leaves
- 1/4 tsp. dried basil leaves
- 2 eggs, well beaten
- 2 cups shredded mozzarella cheese
- 2 tsp. yellow mustard
- 1-8 oz. can crescent rolls

1. **Directions**
   Sauté zucchini and onions in butter in a large skillet for 6-8 minutes or until tender. Some liquid is OK but if your zucchini puts off a lot of liquid (say more than 1/4 cup), pour off excess. Stir in parsley flakes, salt, pepper, garlic powder, oregano and basil. Remove from heat and add eggs, cheese and mustard; stir gently to mix.
2. Separate dough into 8 triangles. Place in ungreased 10-inch pie plate or 11-inch quiche pan; press over bottom and up sides to form crust. Firmly press perforations to seal. Pour zucchini mixture evenly into crust-lined pie plate.
3. Bake at 350º for 25-30 minutes or until mostly set. If necessary, cover edge of crust with strips of foil during last 10 minutes of baking to prevent excessive browning. Remove from oven and let stand, uncovered, for 15 minutes for pie to set up completely before serving.

Zucchini Fries with Onion Dip

Ingredients
- 3 medium zucchini, about 9" to 10" long
- 1 cup Bread Crumbs
- 1/2 cup freshly grated Parmesan cheese
- 1 Tbsp. pizza seasoning or mixed Italian herbs
- 2 large eggs
- 2 Tbsp. cider vinegar
- 2 Tbsp. honey
- 1 Tbsp. prepared mustard
- 1 cup mayo
- 1 Tbsp. butter
- 1 medium sweet onion (half pound)

Zucchini breading
1. Combine the following:
2. 1 cup Panko bread crumbs
3. scant 1/2 cup freshly grated Parmesan cheese
   1 Tbsp. pizza seasoning or mixed Italian herbs
4. Mix until thoroughly combined.

Onion Dip directions
1. Melt 1 Tbsp. butter in a medium-sized frying pan over moderate heat, and add 1 medium sweet onion (about 1/2 pound), sliced.
2. Place the following in a small food processor or blender:
   all of the caramelized onions
   2 Tbsp. cider vinegar
   2 Tbsp. honey
   1 tsp. prepared mustard
3. Process until fairly smooth.
4. Then mix in 1 cup mayo.

Zucchini Directions
1. Cut each zucchini into 3" sticks about the diameter of your finger. Cutting each zucchini into 9 sticks lengthwise, then cutting into 3" lengths, works well.
2. Place the zucchini sticks in a colander over a bowl, and sprinkle with 1 Tbsp. of salt. Let them drain for 1 hour or longer.
3. Rinse them thoroughly; you want to get rid of any excess salt. Then pat them dry.
4. Preheat the oven to 425°. Line a baking sheet with parchment paper.
5. Beat 2 large eggs; Dip each zucchini stick in the egg, then roll it in the crumbs.

Bake the sticks for about 12 minutes, until they're starting to brown. Remove from the oven, and turn them over one by one, or you may be able to turn several at a time using a spatula. Bake for an additional 12 to 16 minutes or so, until golden brown and crisp.

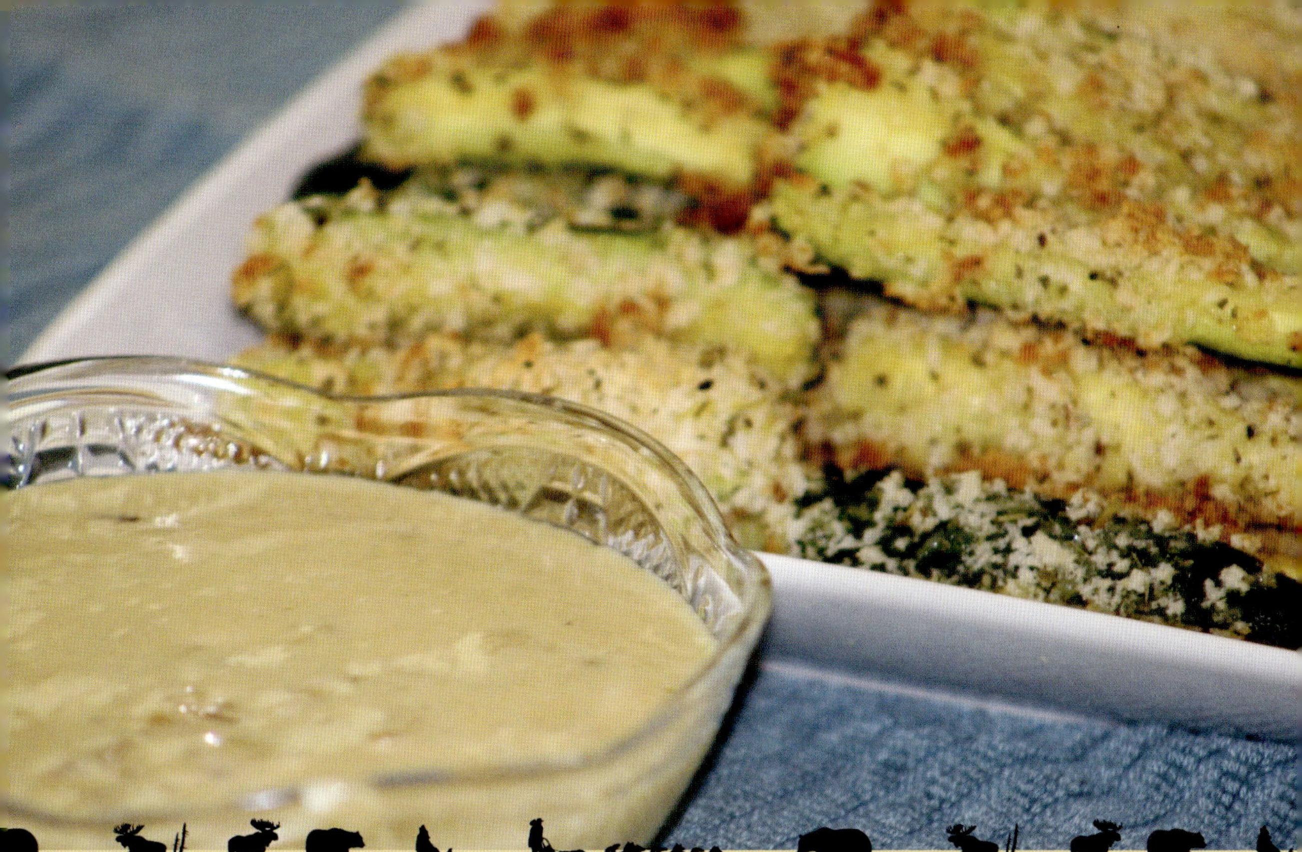

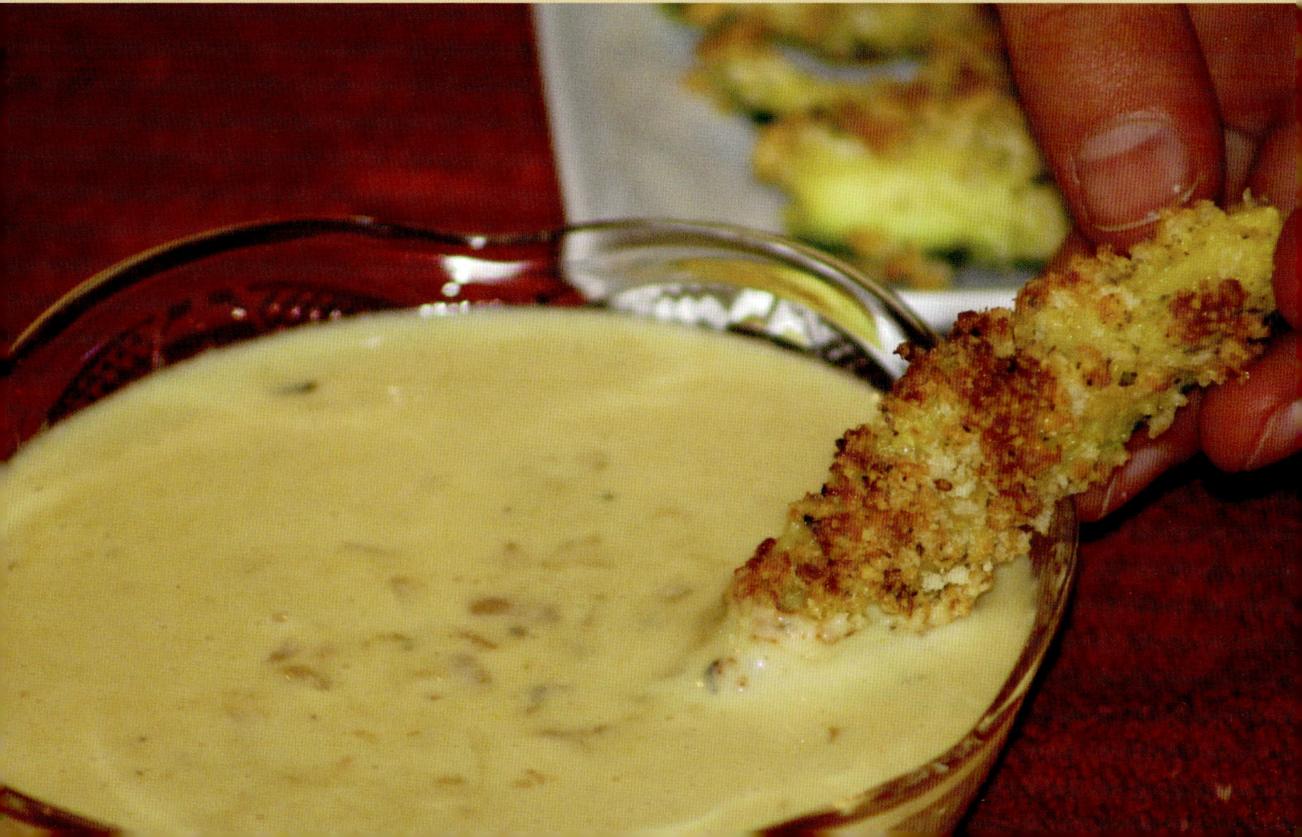

Desserts

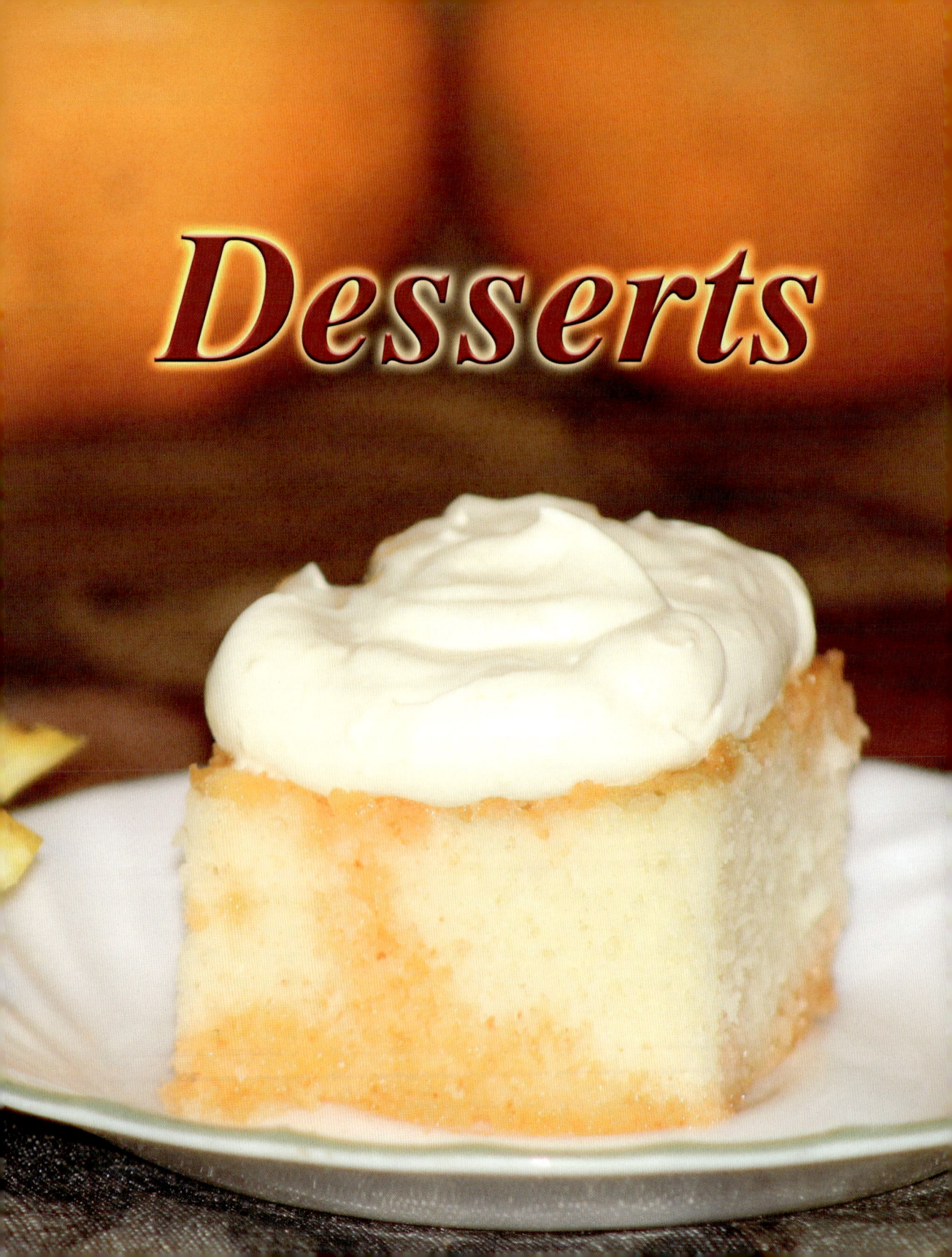

Cheese Tarts

Ingredients
- Pie crust for one double crust 9 inch pie
- 8 oz. cream cheese, room temperature
- 1 cup of sugar
- 1 egg
- 1/2 tsp. lemon extract
- cherry pie filling

The town of Barrow, Alaska, has the longest day and night of any town in the US. The town is 800 miles south of the North Pole. When the sun rises on May 10, it doesn't set again for 3 months. When it sets on November 18th, it will not rise again in Barrow for 2 months.

Directions
1. Preheat oven to 375°. Cut pie crust into 12 circles with a cookie cutter. Butter 24 mini tart pans and place each dough circle inside the tart pan. Alternatively, you could use a mini muffin tin, if you don't have tart pans.
2. In a mixer fitted with a paddle attachment, mix cream cheese, sugar, egg, and vanilla. Cream until there are no lumps.
3. Fill each tart with a teaspoon of the cream cheese mixture. Do not overfill. You want your tart filled less than halfway TOTAL with cream cheese and cherries. If you overfill, it will make a mess.
4. Bake each tart for about 10 minutes, until pie crust edges are lightly browned. Enjoy!

Orange Creamsicle Cookies

Ingredients:
- 1 1/4 cup Sugar
- 1/2 cup butter, softened
- 4 oz. cream cheese, softened
- 1 egg
- 1 tsp. vanilla
- 2 Tbsp. finely grated orange rind
- 1/4 cup freshly squeezed orange juice
- 2 3/4 cup flour
- 1 tsp. baking soda
- 1 tsp. cream of tartar
- 1/4 tsp. salt
- 1 1/2 cup white chocolate chips

Directions:
1. Preheat oven to 350º. In the bowl of an electric mixer, cream together sugar, butter, cream cheese, egg, vanilla, orange rind, and orange juice for 1-2 minutes, until well combined.
2. In a separate bowl, stir together flour, baking soda, cream of tartar and salt. Add to creamed mixture and mix until combined. Stir in white chocolate chips.
3. Scoop onto a greased cookie sheet and bake for approximately 8 minutes, or just until done, so they stay nice and chewy and soft.
4. Let cool on the cookie sheet for a few minutes, then remove to a cooling rack to cool completely. Store in an airtight container so they stay soft.

Banana Cookies

Ingredients
- 1 cup sugar
- 1/2 cup unsalted butter, softened
- 1/2 cup shortening
- 1 tsp. Vanilla extract
- 2 eggs
- 3 ripe mashed bananas (about 1 cup)
- 1/2 cup buttermilk
- 1 1/2 tsp. Baking soda
- 1/2 tsp. Salt
- 3 1/4 cups all purpose flour

Directions
1. Preheat oven to 350º.
2. In a large bowl, cream together sugar, butter, shortening, and vanilla until light and fluffy.
3. Mix in eggs and bananas.
4. Blend in buttermilk.
5. Add the dry ingredients until just combined.
6. Do not overbeat. It will be a sticky batter.
7. Drop by tablespoons onto a greased cookie sheet.
8. Bake 9-10 minutes until slightly golden.
9. Spread banana frosting over cooled cookies and serve.

Peanut Butter Teddies

Ingredients
- 1 can (14 oz.) sweetened condensed milk
- 1 cup creamy peanut butter
- 1 tsp. vanilla extract
- 1 egg
- 2 cups all-purpose flour
- 2 tsp. baking soda
- 1/2 tsp. salt
- 72 miniature semisweet chocolate chips

Directions
1. In a large bowl, beat the milk, peanut butter, vanilla and egg until smooth. Combine the flour, baking soda and salt; add to peanut butter mixture and mix well.
2. For each pair, shape the dough into one 1-in. ball, one 3/4-in. ball, six 1/2-in. balls and one 1/4-in. ball. On an ungreased baking sheet, slightly flatten the 1-in. ball to form the body. Place the 3/4-in. ball above body for head. For limbs, place four 1/2-in. balls next to the body.
3. For nose, place the 1/4-in. ball in the center of the heat. Add two chocolate chips for eyes. Bake at 350° for 6-8 minutes or until lightly browned. Cool on baking sheets. Yield: approximately 2 dozen.

Desiree got tired of making teddies, so she made other creative shapes.

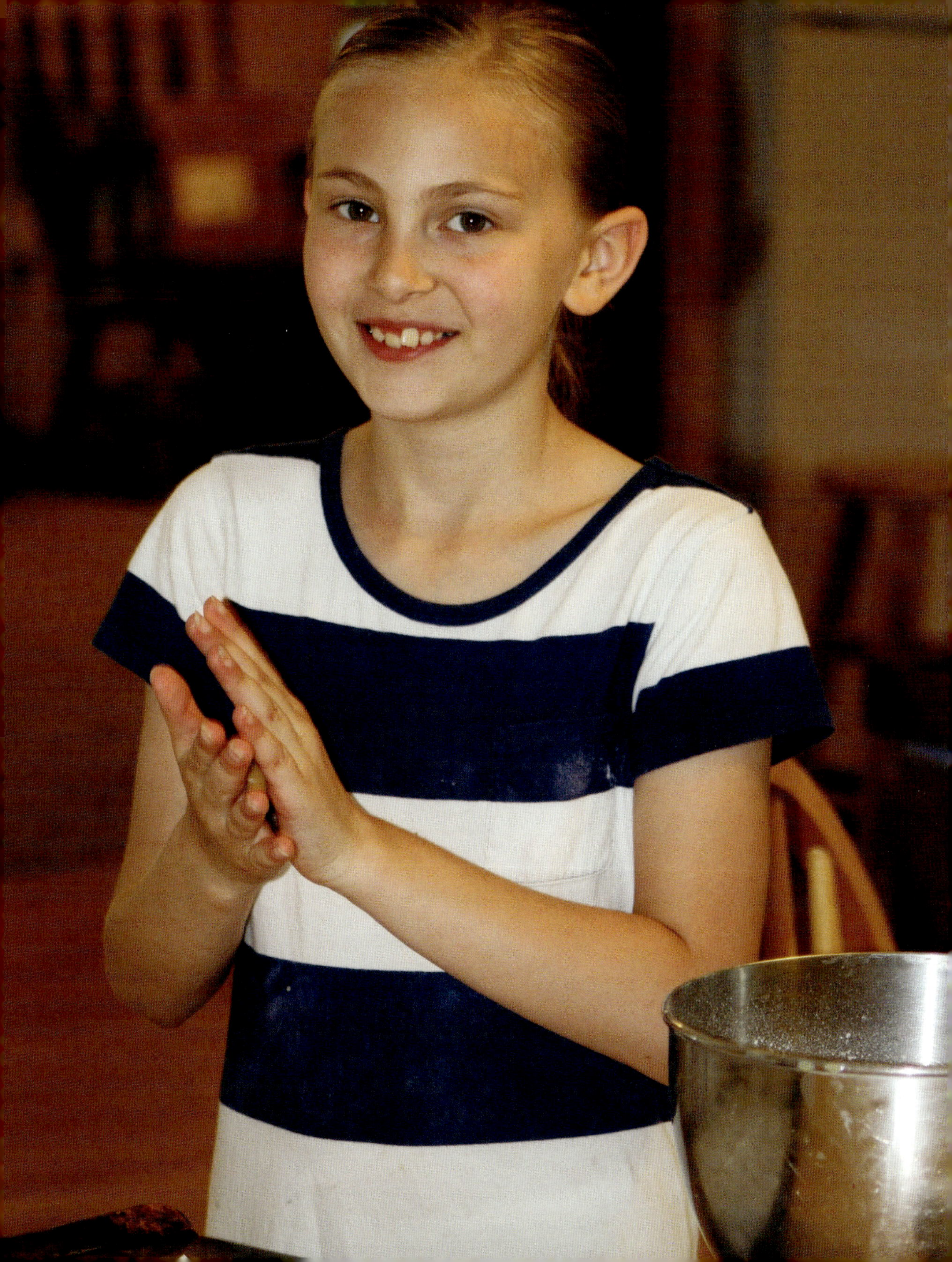

Bigfoot Cookies

Ingredients
- 3 eggs
- 1 cup brown sugar
- 1 cup sugar
- 1 tsp. vanilla
- 2 tsp. baking soda
- 1/4 lb. butter
- 1 1/2 cups peanut butter
- 4 1/2 cups oatmeal
- 1/2 cups M&M candy
- 1 tsp. corn syrup

Directions
1. Mix in order.
2. Bake on greased cookie sheet at 350º.
3. Keep your eye on cookies, don't overbake, should be ready around 8 minutes.

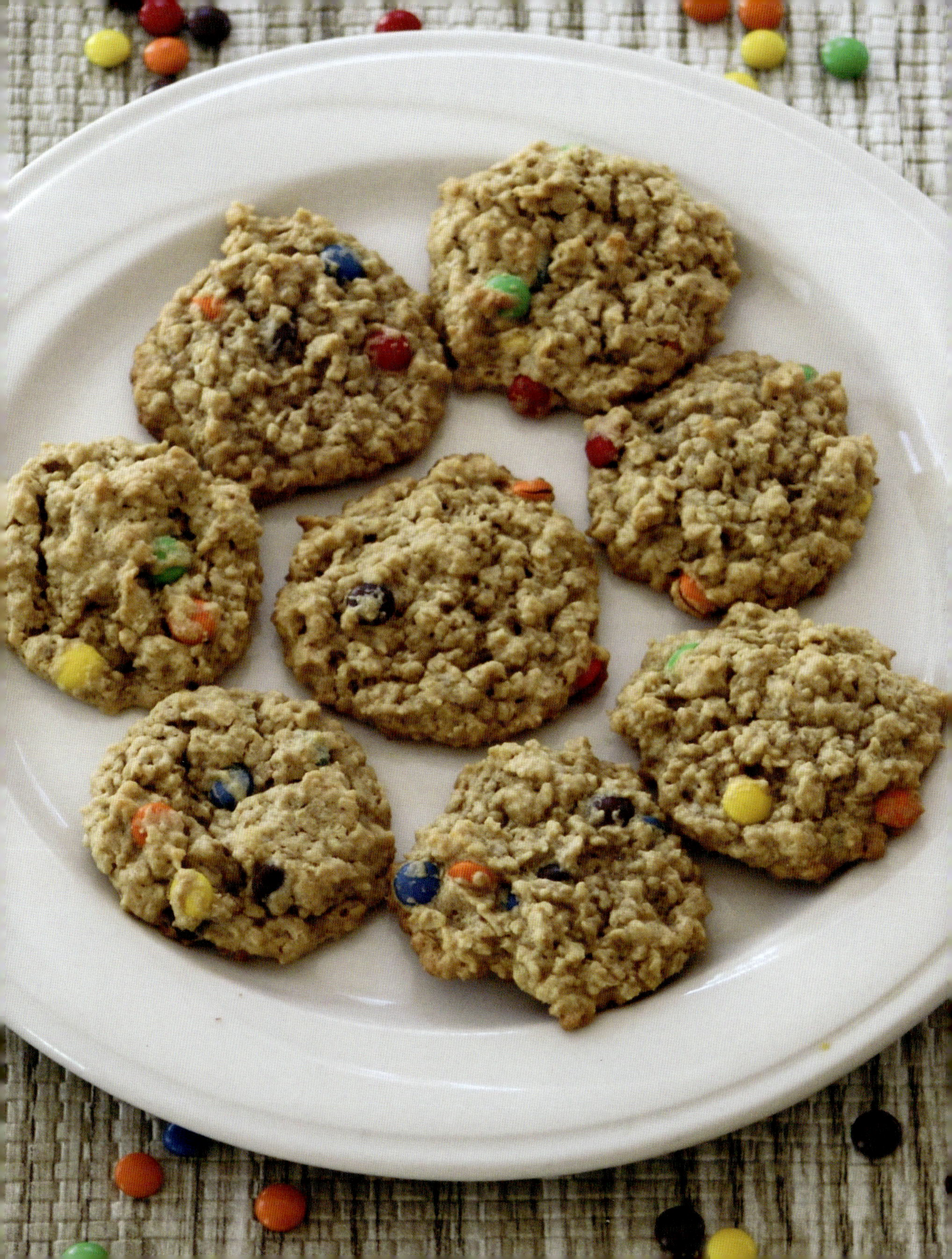

Alcan Highway Cookies

Ingredients

- 3/4 cup granulated sugar
- 3/4 cup packed brown sugar
- 1 cup butter or margarine, softened
- 1 tsp. vanilla
- 1 egg
- 2 1/4 cups all purpose flour
- 1 tsp. baking soda
- 1/2 tsp. salt
- 1 cup coarsely chopped nuts
- 1 package (12 ounces) semisweet chocolate chips (2 cups)

THIS IS MATT'S RECIPE, AND MADE BY MATT

Directions

Note: We like to think these cookies turn out best if mixed and baked while you are actually driving on the Alcan (Alaska) highway. In a pinch you can just drive around the block while making them, or in worst case scenario, stationary in your kitchen at home. We recommend having a second person drive while you make the cookies, please don't do both at once, it's worse than texting while driving.

1. Heat oven to 375°.
2. Mix sugars, butter, vanilla and egg in large bowl. Stir in flour, baking soda and salt (dough will be stiff). Stir in nuts and chocolate chips.
3. Drop dough by rounded tablespoon about 2 inches apart onto ungreased cookie sheet.
4. Bake 8 to 10 minutes or until light brown (centers will be soft). Cool slightly; remove from cookie sheet. Cool on wire rack.

Matt felt a little seasick when he mixed up these cookies while I was driving.

The cookies got a little lopsided. This is the second batch, the first batch he did looked much worse. I guess they are not bad for being made while driving down the highway.

Peanut Butter Winkies

Ingredients
- 1/2 cup creamy peanut butter
- 2 oz. cream cheese, softened
- 3 Tbsp. maple syrup
- 1 tsp. vanilla extract
- 1/4 cup melted coconut oil
- Melted semisweet chocolate for drizzling

Directions
1. Place peanut butter, cream cheese, and maple syrup in a medium bowl. Using a handheld electric mixer, beat on medium speed until creamy. Mix in vanilla and coconut oil until a very soft dough forms. Place dough in freezer to chill 5-10 minutes until it just starts to solidify.
2. Once dough is thickened, roll dough into 1-in balls and place on a parchment paper-lined sheet. Chill winkies in freezer 5-10 minutes or until firm.
3. Remove from freezer and drizzle with melted chocolate. Return to freezer for an additional 5 minutes or until chocolate hardens. Store them in refrigerator until ready to serve.
4. You can store winkies in refrigerator up to 1 week. May also be frozen up to 2 months.

Chocolate Peanut Butter Bites

These chocolate peanut butter no-bake energy bites taste just like a cookie, although they are full of protein and naturally sweetened.

Ingredients
- 1 cup (dry) oatmeal
- 2/3 cup toasted unsweetened coconut flakes
- 1/2 cup peanut butter
- 1/2 cup ground flax seed
- 1/3 cup honey or agave nectar
- 1/4 cup unsweetened cocoa powder
- 1 Tbsp. chia seeds (optional)
- 1 tsp. vanilla extract

Alaska become a state on January 3, 1959. It was the 49th state to join the Union, before statehood it was a US territory.

Directions
1. Stir all ingredients together in a medium bowl until thoroughly mixed.
2. Cover and chill in the refrigerator for at least half an hour, to make the mix easier to handle and mold.
3. Once chilled, roll into balls of whatever size you would like. (Mine were about 1" in diameter.) Store in an airtight container and keep refrigerated for up to 1 week.

*If the mix seems to dry, add in an extra tablespoon or two of honey or peanut butter. If the mix seems too wet (which may happen if you use natural peanut butter), add extra oatmeal.

Strawberry and White Chocolate Chip Cookies

Ingredients
- 1 box strawberry cake mix
- 1 stick (8 Tbsp.) butter, melted
- 1 egg
- 1 tsp. vanilla
- 4 oz. cream cheese, room temperature
- 3/4 cup white chocolate chips
- 3/4 cup M&Ms

Directions
1. Combine butter, egg, vanilla, and cream cheese in a bowl. Mix together thoroughly.
2. Add cake mix, half of the box at a time, mixing until well combined.
3. Stir in chips and candies by hand.
4. Refrigerate for at least one hour and then roll dough into 1 inch balls.
5. Preheat oven to 350º.
6. Place dough balls onto parchment lined baking sheet and bake for 9 minutes - you don't want the cookies to brown at all! Set a timer.
7. Let cookies cool on a baking sheet for several minutes before removing to a wire rack to cool completely.
8. Cookies can be stored in an airtight container for 4-5 days.

Polar Bear Paws

Ingredients

Caramel:
- 2 cups sugar
- 3/4 cup dark corn syrup
- 3/4 cup butter 2 cups whipping cream (divided)
- 1 tsp. vanilla
- 1 cup peanuts (I used lightly salted)

Coating:
- 16 oz. vanilla candy coating (or almond bark)

Directions
1. Line a cookie sheet with parchment paper and set aside.
2. Mix sugar, corn syrup, butter, and 1 cup whipping cream in a 4 quart pan and bring to a boil over medium heat. Stir constantly.
3. Once it comes to a boil, heat the other cup of whipping cream in the microwave for 1 minute until hot. Gradually add the cream to the ingredients cooking in the pan, stirring constantly. (add it slowly so the caramel mixture never stops boiling)
4. Continue stirring and it will begin to thicken and darken in color. Cook until it reaches about 242 degrees (soft ball stage). You can do the cold water test by drizzling a little of the caramel into cold water, let it sit for a few seconds and then pull it out and if it can hold the shape of a ball then it's done. If not, keep cooking and repeat the test. (This cooking process to get it to the right temperature could take up to 20 - 25 minutes. Just keep stirring over the medium heat.)
5. When it reaches the soft ball stage or 242 degrees, remove from heat and stir in vanilla. Then fold in the peanuts. Pour into a bowl to cool for about 30 minutes, stirring every few minutes to cool quicker.
6. Spoon onto parchment paper in tablespoon size mounds. Place in the fridge for about 30 minutes until set.
7. Melt vanilla candy coating in the microwave on low for 30 second increments. Stir until melted and smooth. Dip the caramel cluster into the white chocolate with a fork allowing the excess chocolate to drip off. (I use a plastic fork with the middle tines broken out. This works great for letting the excess chocolate to drip back into the bowl) Place back onto the parchment lined pan to set up. They can be refrigerated to set up faster.

Shane's Favorite

Survival Tip: Eating raw polar bear meat will stave off scurvy, although I don't know anyone personally who has done this.

Chocolate Surprise Cookies

Ingredients:
- 1 1/2 cups all-purpose flour
- 1/2 cup unsweetened cocoa powder
- 1/2 tsp. baking soda
- 1/2 cup white sugar
- 1/2 cup packed brown sugar
- 1/2 cup soft margarine
- 1/4 cup peanut butter
- 1 tsp. vanilla extract
- 1 egg
- 3/4 cup peanut butter

Directions
1. In small bowl blend flour, cocoa and baking soda. Mix until well blended.
2. In large bowl beat white and brown sugars, butter or margarine and 1/4 cup peanut butter, until light and fluffy. Add vanilla and egg, beat. Stir in flour mixture until blended. Set aside.
3. To make Filling: Combine confectioner's sugar and 3/4 cup peanut butter. Blend well.
4. Roll filling into 30 1-inch balls. For each cookie, with floured hands, shape about 1 tablespoon of dough around 1 peanut butter ball, covering completely. Place 2 inches apart on an ungreased cookie sheet. Flatten with glass dipped in white sugar.
5. Bake at 375º for 7-9 minutes. When cookies are done, they should be set and slightly cracked.

Almond Joy Energy Bites

Ingredients
- 12 oz. (about 2 cups, loosely-packed) dates (you may need to soak dates first to soften them)
- 2 cups almonds
- 1/2 cup shredded coconut
- 1/2 cup unsweetened cocoa powder
- 1 Tbsp. coconut oil
- 1 Tbsp. vanilla extract
- 1/2 tsp. almond extract (optional)

These are excellent to take along hunting or hiking.

Directions
1. Add dates and remaining ingredients to a food processor. Pulse a few times to combine, then use a rubber spatula to scrape the sides of the bowl. Blend the mixture for about 3 minutes, or until the mixture has moved past the crumbly stage and begins to clump and stick to the sides of the food processor.
2. Use a spoon or small cookie scoop to measure out a tablespoon of dough (or your desired size) and roll it into a ball. If desired, roll the ball in a bowl of coconut flakes. Repeat with the remaining dough. (Or, you can flatten the dough into the bottom of an 8x8-inch parchment-lined baking dish, then cut it into bars.)
3. Store the energy bites in an airtight container for up to 2 weeks.

Avalanche Bars

Ingredients
- 1 (12 oz.) bag white chocolate chips
- 2 heaping Tbsp. creamy peanut butter
- 3 cups crispy rice cereal
- 1/2 cup mini chocolate chips
- 1 1/2 cups miniature marshmallows

Avalanches are triggered for safety purposes along mountain passes near highways. This is done by shooting artillery shells into the mountain side (the road is closed first).

Instructions
1. In a large, microwave-safe bowl, melt white chocolate chips with peanut butter for about 40 seconds.
2. Just stir together until all the white chocolate chips are melted. Add crispy rice cereal to mixture and wait about 10-15 minutes until the mix has reached room temp.
3. Add mini chocolate chips and marshmallows. Stir until well combined.
4. Grease a 9"x13" baking pan. Press mixture down into the pan with a greased spoon or hand (but don't smash the rice cereal).
5. Place in the fridge for about 30 minutes or until hardened. Cut into squares and serve!

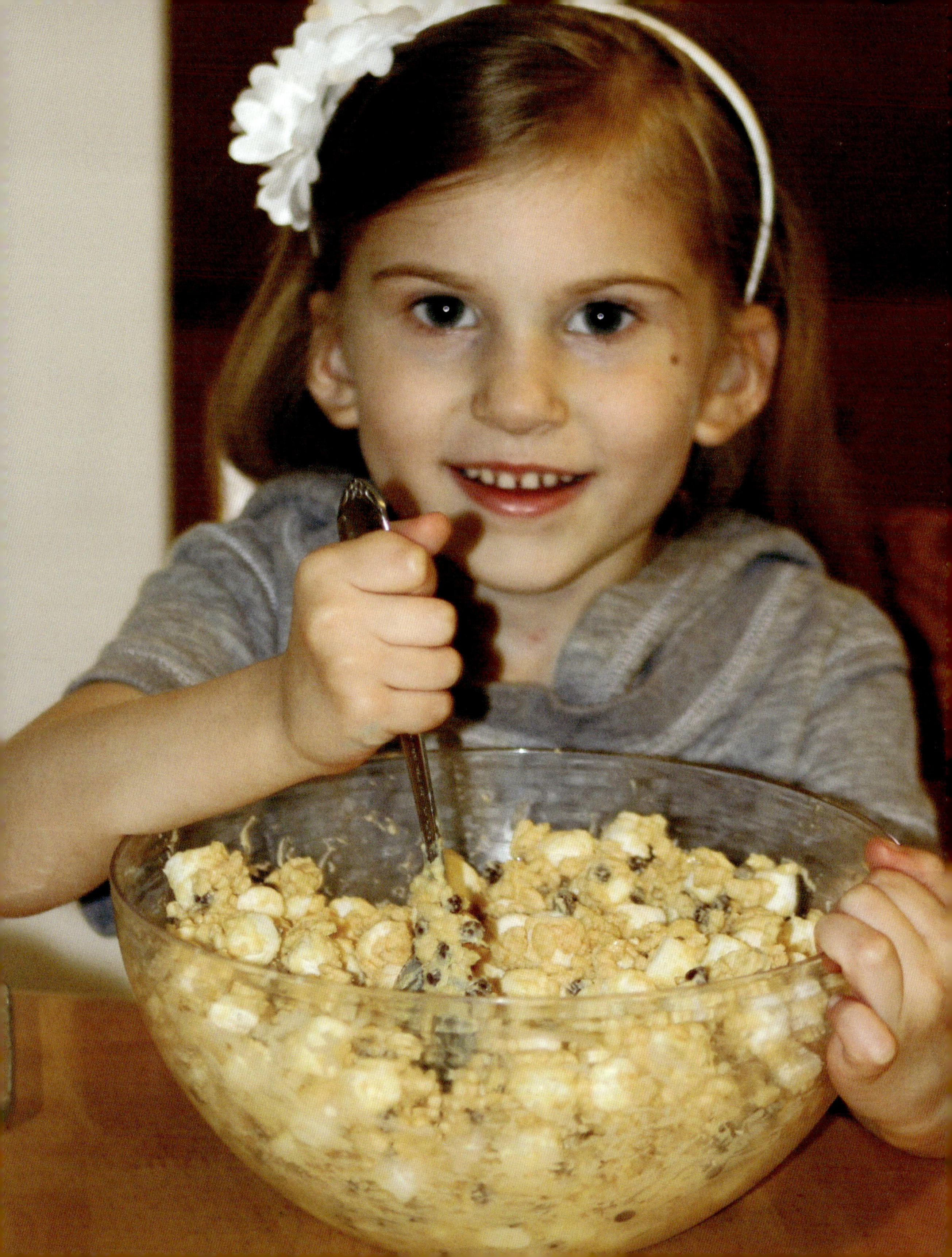

Apple Snickerdoodle Bars

Ingredients
- 1/4 cup room temperature butter
- 1 cup light brown sugar, packed
- 1 egg
- 1 tsp. vanilla extract
- 1 cup flour
- 1 tsp. baking powder
- 1/2 tsp. salt
- 1 cup of tart apples, peeled and chopped
- 2 Tbsp. granulated sugar
- 1 1/2 tsp. ground cinnamon

It's a bad deal to have deer or rabbits in your garden, but a moose will clean out a whole garden in one morning!

1. **Directions**
   Preheat the oven to 350° and put in a 8"×8" pan. (You can double this recipe and put it in a 9"×13" pan as well.) Spray the sling with non-stick spray.
2. In your mixer, whip together your butter and brown sugar until light. Add the egg and vanilla and mix well. Add the flour, salt, baking powder, and mix until just combined. Add the chopped apples at the very end and stir by hand into the mixture.
3. Press into your prepared pan. Slightly damp, clean hands work best for this. Mix the cinnamon and sugar together and sprinkle over the top.
4. Bake for 25-30 minutes until a toothpick inserted into the center comes out clean. Cool and serve. Enjoy!

S'mores Cookie Bars

Ingredients

Graham Cracker Layer:
- 2 cups of graham cracker crumbs (About 10 cracker sheets)
- 6 tablespoons melted butter
- 1/4 cup granulated sugar
- 1 egg white

Chocolate Layer
- 1 1/2 cups melted milk chocolate chips

Marshmallow Layer
- 3/4 cup marshmallow crème
- about half a bag of marshmallows

Directions

1. Preheat your oven to 350°. Spray a 9"×9" baking pan with cooking spray. You must not skip this step or your bars will not come out of the pan!
2. Crush graham crackers into fine crumbs using a food processor. Place them in a large bowl. Add the sugar, melted butter, and egg white and mix together until well combined. Press into the bottom of your prepared pan. Bake for 10 minutes and remove from the oven and cool completely.
3. When graham cracker layer is cool, melt your chocolate chips either in the microwave (30 seconds at a time, stirring in between, careful not to burn) or in a double broiler. Once chocolate is melted, mix well, and spread over the top of the graham cracker layer. Place pan in the refrigerator, and cool completely until the chocolate has hardened.
4. Once chocolate has hardened, turn your oven up to the broiler setting and put your oven rack in the highest position. Spread a thin layer of marshmallow crème over the top of the chocolate. This is the "glue" that will hold your marshmallows in place. Then neatly and evenly place the marshmallows as close together as possible over the entire pan leaving as few gaps as possible. This part takes patience if you want them to look pretty.
5. Place the pan under the broiler on the top rack and leave the oven door cracked open and watch the marshmallows toast. This will take under a minute. Watch the whole time and remove as soon as the tops are golden.
6. Put the pan back into the fridge until completely cool and then slice and serve. This recipe can easily be doubled and put into a 9"×13" inch pan.

Oreo Bars

Ingredients

For crust:
- 24 Oreo Cookies, crushed into very fine crumbs
- 1/4 cup melted butter

For cheesecake:
- 2 packages (8 oz each) cream cheese, at room temperature
- 2/3 cup sugar
- 2 eggs
- 1 Tbsp. vanilla extract
- 1/3 cup sour cream
- About 10 Oreo Cookies, coarsely chopped/crushed
- Hot Fudge Sauce, for drizzling on top, optional but recommended

Directions

1. Preheat oven to 325º. Line an 8"x8" baking pan with foil, extending the sides of the foil over the edges of the pan. Mist the foil with cooking spray and set aside.
2. In a medium bowl, stir together the finely crushed Oreo crumbs and the melted butter until combined and moistened. Press into the prepared pan in an even, single layer and bake for approx. 12 minutes. Remove from the oven but keep the oven on.
3. While crust bakes, prepare your filling. In the bowl of a stand mixer, combine the cream cheese and sugar and beat on medium for about 2 minutes or until combined and fluffy. Add in the eggs, one at a time, beating very well after each addition. Beat in the vanilla and sour cream for about 1 minute or until the cheesecake is very light and smooth. Beat in the remaining coarsely crushed Oreo Cookies.
4. Spread the mixture into the baking dish and smooth out the top. Bake for approx. 35-40 minutes or until the edges are set, the top is very light golden brown and the center is just about set and only a little bit jiggly. Cool completely at room temperature and then once cool, refrigerate for at least 3 hours, preferably overnight, before cutting into bars. Drizzle the room temperature hot fudge on top of the bars just before serving.

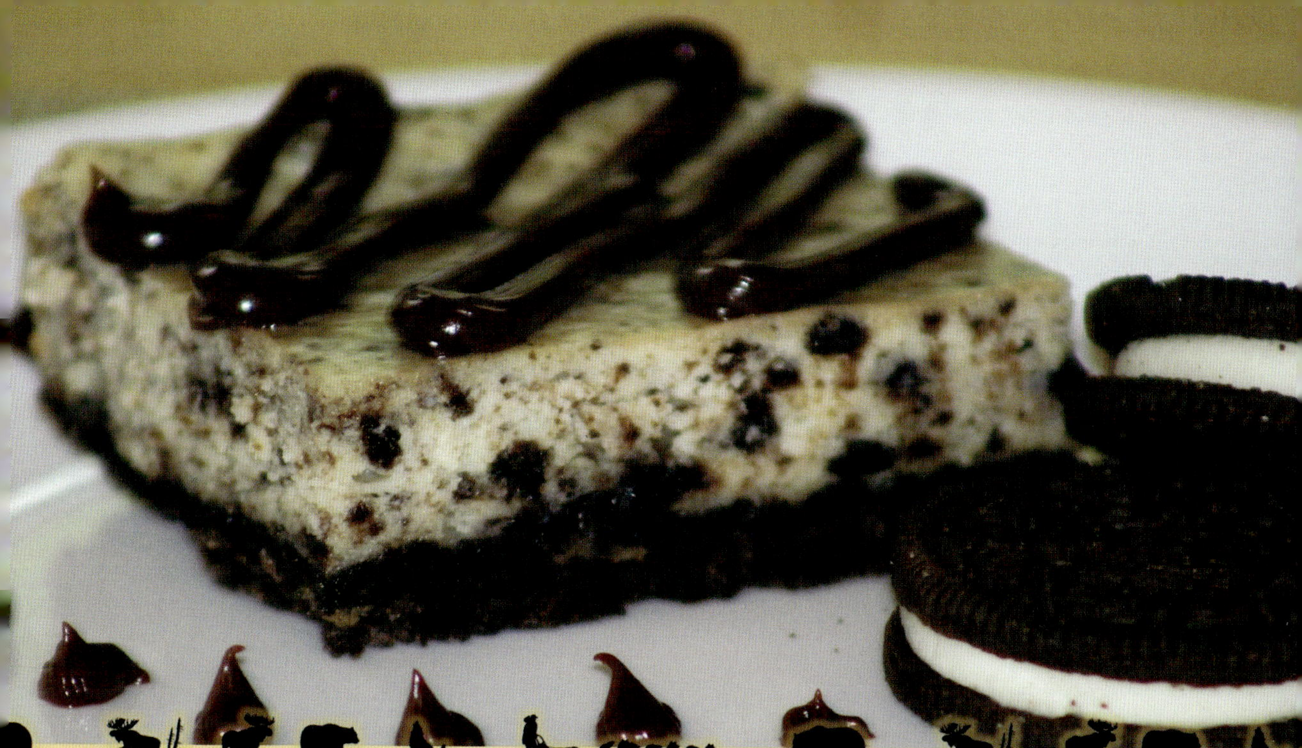

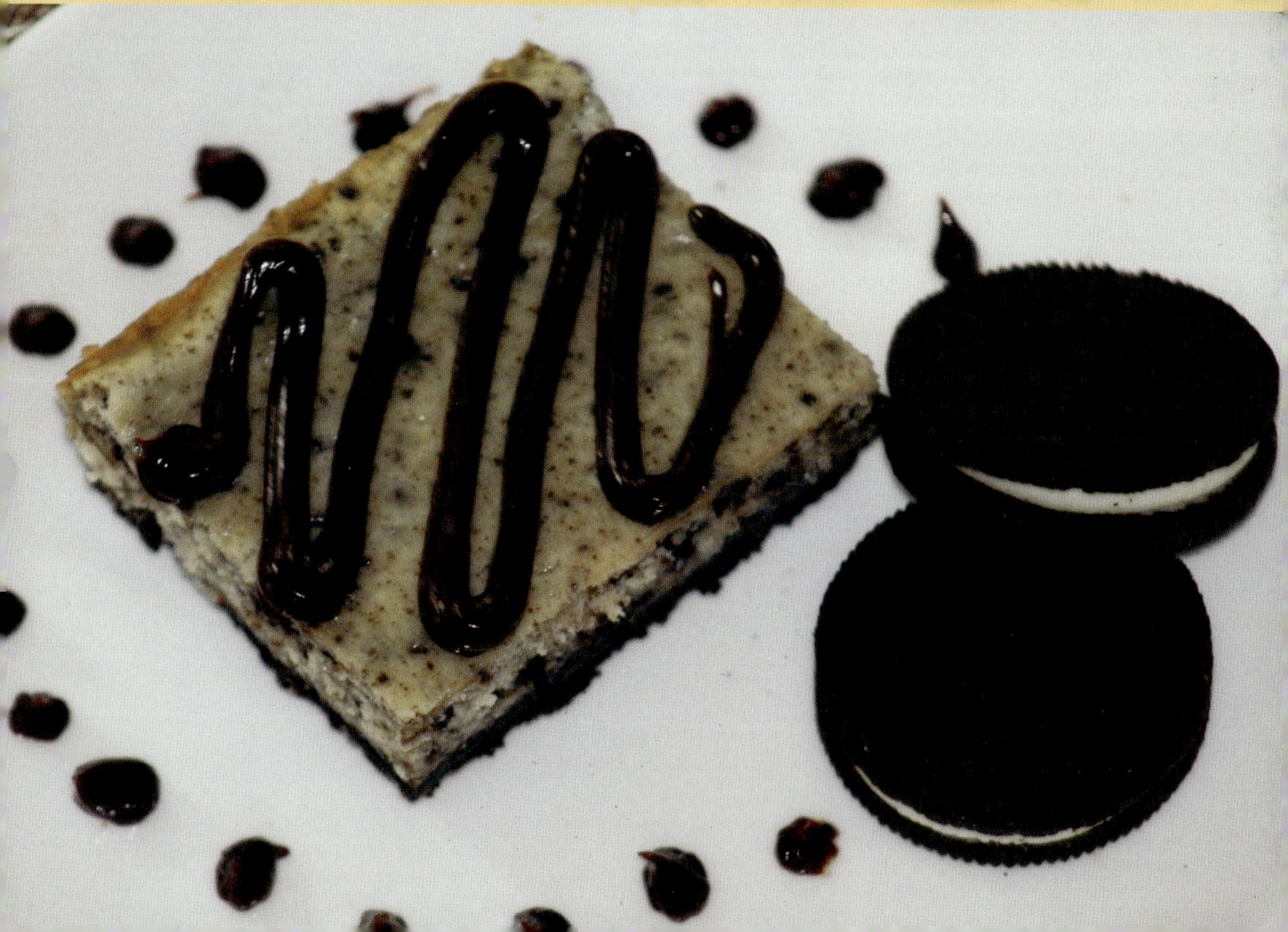

M & M Dream Bars

Ingredients
- 2 cups oatmeal
- 1 cup brown sugar
- 1 tsp. soda
- 1/2 tsp. salt
- 1 1/2 cup flour
- 1 cup melted butter
- 1 can sweetened condensed milk
- 1/3 cup peanut butter
- 1 cup chocolate chips
- 1 cup M&M candy

Directions
1. Combine oatmeal, brown sugar, soda, salt, and flour. Add melted butter to make crumbs. Reserve one cup for topping.
2. Press remaining crumbs into a 9"x13" pan.
3. Bake at 375º for 12 minutes. Combine condensed milk, peanut butter, and spread over the baked crust.
4. Sprinkle with M&M's, chocolate chips, and crumbs on top of the peanut butter mixture.
5. Bake at 20 minutes or until golden brown.

Chocolate Revel Bars

Ingredients
Cookie Base:
- 1 cup butter
- 2 cups brown sugar
- 2 eggs
- 2 tsp. vanilla
- 2 1/2 cups sifted flour
- 1 tsp. baking soda
- 1 tsp. salt
- 3 cups quick oatmeal

Chocolate Filling:
- 12 oz. package semi-sweet chocolate chips
- 15 oz. can sweetened condensed milk
- 2 Tbsp. butter
- 1/2 tsp. salt
- 1 cup chopped walnuts (opt.)
- 2 tsp. vanilla

Cookie Base:
1. Cream butter and sugar until light and fluffy. Mix in eggs and vanilla. Sift together the flour, soda and salt. Mix quick oats with flour mixture. Add dry ingredients to the creamed mixture.
2. Spread 2/3 of the oatmeal mixture in the bottom of a 15x10x1-inch jelly roll pan.
3. Cover with the following chocolate filling. Dot with remaining oatmeal. Bake in 350º oven for 25 to 30 minutes.

Chocolate Filling:
1. Mix chocolate chips, sweetened condensed milk, butter and salt together in the top of a double boiler and melt.
2. When smooth, add the nuts and vanilla.

Chocolate Peanut Butter Dream Bars

Ingredients

- 1 16 oz. package peanut butter sandwich cookies, divided
- 4 Tbsp. butter (1/2 stick) butter, melted
- 4 oz. cream cheese, room temperature
- 1/2 cup confectioners' sugar
- 1/3 cup creamy peanut butter
- 1 8 oz. container Cool Whip, divided
- 1 3.9 oz. package instant chocolate Jello Pudding Mix
- 1 1/2 cups milk
- 1/2 cup milk chocolate & peanut butter chips OR 1/4 cup milk chocolate chips + 1/4 cup peanut butter chips

Directions

1. Preheat the oven to 350º.
2. In a blender or food processor, finely crush 24 of the cookies.
3. In a medium bowl, mix together the melted butter and finely crushed cookies until well moistened.
4. Press into an ungreased 8"x8" inch baking dish.
5. Bake for 10 minutes.
6. Allow crust to cool completely before proceeding.
7. In the meantime, mix the package of pudding with the 1 1/2 cups of milk in a small bowl.
8. In a mixing bowl, beat cream cheese, confectioners' sugar, and peanut butter together.
9. Fold in 1 cup of the Cool Whip and mix until well blended.
10. Spread the chocolate pudding over the cooled crust.
11. Place dollops of cream cheese mixture over the pudding layer and with a spatula, gently spread to completely cover.
12. Spread remaining Cool Whip over the cream cheese.
13. Refrigerate two hours.
14. In a plastic bag, break up the 8 remaining cookies.
15. Sprinkle the cookies and chocolate / peanut butter chips over the top just before serving.

Triple Chocolate Cherry Bars

Ingredients
- 6 oz. bittersweet chocolate chips (about 1 cup)
- 1/2 cup unsalted
- 2 eggs, room temperature
- 3/4 cup sugar
- 1/4 tsp. salt
- 2 tsp. vanilla extract
- 2/3 cup all purpose flour
- 4 oz. white chocolate chips (about 2/3 cup)
- 1/2 cup mini semi-sweet chocolate chips
- 10 oz. jar maraschino cherries, drained, halved, and patted dry

At 20,310 feet, Denali (located in Alaska) is the highest mountain peak in North America. Originally named Mount McKinley, the name was officially changed to Denali on August 28, 2015.

Directions
1. Preheat oven to 325°.
2. Spray an 8"x8" or 9"x9" pan with cooking spray and line with parchment paper. Let paper extend over two sides for easy removal of brownies.
3. Melt bittersweet chocolate and butter together in a microwave safe container. Heat on high for 30 second, stir. Repeat. Let sit for a few minutes and stir again. Chocolate should be smooth and completely melted. If not, heat on 50% power for in 15 second intervals until melted.
4. Beat eggs and sugar together in a medium bowl with a fork.
5. Mix in salt and vanilla extract. Add in melted chocolate mixture.
6. Add flour just until combined.
7. Combine in white chocolate chips, mini chocolate chips, and cherries.
8. Pour into prepared pan and smooth top.
9. Bake for 25-30 minutes or until center has set.

Chocolate Chip Skillet Brownie

Ingredients

Brownie Batter:
- 1/3 cup butter, melted
- 1/2 cup brown sugar
- 1/3 cup white sugar
- 1/2 cup unsweetened cocoa powder
- 1 large egg
- 1 tsp. pure vanilla extract
- 1/2 tsp. salt
- 1/4 cup all-purpose flour
- 2 Tbsp. warm water

Cookie Dough:
- 1/4 cup butter, softened
- 1/4 cup light brown sugar
- 1/4 cup granulated sugar
- 1 large egg
- 1 tsp. pure vanilla extract
- 2/3 cup all-purpose flour
- 1/8 tsp. baking soda
- Pinch salt
- 1/3 cup dark/semi-sweet chocolate chips

Directions

1. Heat the oven to 350°. Lightly grease an 9" cast iron skillet or round baking pan with non-stick spray.
2. In a medium-sized bowl, whisk the butter and sugars together well until the sugar has dissolved. Add the cocoa powder, whisking until dissolved and smooth.
3. Beat in the egg and vanilla until well incorporated (about a minute). Fold the flour and salt through until the better is smooth and thick. Pour in the water and lightly mix it through until the batter is smooth (it will still be quite thick). Set aside.

For The Cookie Dough:

1. In a separate medium-sized bowl, beat the butter and sugars together until light and fluffy. Add the egg and vanilla, beating until smooth. Add in the flour, baking soda and salt, folding the dry ingredients through until a cookie dough forms. Fold in half of the chocolate chips; set aside.

Assemble:

1. Pour the brownie batter into the skillet (or pan) and spread out evenly with a spatula (or the back of a metal spoon). Scoop the cookie dough into the brownie batter; sprinkle with the remaining chocolate chips; and bake for 30-35 minutes, or until the cookie is golden and the edges are set and pulling away from the sides of the pan. Do not over bake or it will be dry instead of moist and fudge-like.
2. Allow to cool in the pan for about 10 minutes and serve hot.

Impossible Pumpkin Cupcakes

Ingredients
- 2/3 cup all purpose flour
- 15 oz pumpkin puree
- 3/4 cup sugar
- 2 large eggs
- 1 tsp. vanilla
- 3/4 cup evaporated milk
- 2 tsp. pumpkin pie spice
- 1/4 tsp. salt
- 1/4 tsp. baking powder
- 1/4 tsp. baking soda
- Whipped cream

Directions
1. Line a 12-cup muffin tin with paper or silicone liners.
2. Preheat oven to 350º.
3. In a bowl, whisk together flour, baking powder, baking soda, salt and pumpkin pie spice.
4. In a large bowl, whisk together pumpkin puree, sugar, eggs, vanilla and evaporated milk until well combined.
5. Add in dry ingredients and whisk until no streaks of flour remain and batter is smooth.
6. Fill each muffin cup with approximately ⅓ cup of batter.
7. Bake for 20 minutes and let cool for 20 minutes.
8. Remove cupcakes from pan and chill in the fridge for 30 minutes.
9. Top with whipped cream and sprinkle with more pumpkin pie spice or cinnamon on top and before serving.

Orange Creamsicle Cake

Kallia's Favorite

Ingredients:
- 1 (18.25 oz.) package orange cake mix
- Eggs, oil, and water called for on cake mix box
- 1 (3 oz.) package orange Jello
- 1 cup boiling water
- 1 (3.4 oz.) package instant vanilla pudding mix
- 1 cup milk
- 1 (8 oz.) container vanilla Cool Whip, thawed

Directions
1. Prepare and bake cake mix according to package directions for a 9"x13" pan. Poke holes in cake while still hot with the round handle of a wooden spoon.
2. In a medium bowl, stir together Jello and boiling water. Pour liquid Jello over cake while hot. Cool cake completely, then refrigerate for at least an hour.
3. In a medium bowl, make instant vanilla pudding with milk. Gently fold in Cool Whip. Spread evenly over cake. Refrigerate cake for another hour before serving.

Pistachio Cake

Ingredients
- 1 box white cake mix
- 5 eggs
- 1/2 cup milk
- 1/2 cup oil
- 1/2 cup water
- 2 boxes pistachio pudding

Directions
Mix everything together, and bake at 350º till done.

Icing:
- 1 box pistachio pudding
- 1/2 pint heavy whipping cream
- 8 oz. cool whip

Mix together, and spread on top of cooled cake.

Desiree's Favorite

Earthquake Cake

Ingredients
- 1 cup chopped pecans
- 2 cups sweetened flaked coconut
- 1 box chocolate cake mix
- Eggs, oil and water for cake mix
- 1/2 cup butter, melted
- 1 8 oz. package cream cheese, at room temperature
- 3 cups powdered sugar
- 1 cup semi-sweet chocolate chips

Directions
1. Spray a 13"x9" (3 quart) pan with cooking spray. Scatter pecans and coconut evenly into pan. Prepare cake batter following instructions on box and pour over pecans and coconut.
2. Combine melted butter and cream cheese in a medium-sized bowl then beat with an electric mixer until smooth. Add powdered sugar, one cup at a time, and beat on low until smooth and creamy.
3. Dallop heaping tablespoons of the cream cheese mixture evenly onto cake batter. Sprinkle cake with chocolate chips. Bake at 350º for 40-45 minutes or until set.

Yes-we live in an earthquake zone! It is not uncommon to feel the ground shake, and then it's time to hang on for the ride!

No Bake Strawberry Delight

Ingredients
- 1 box (3.4 oz) vanilla instant pudding
- 1 1/2 cups milk
- 1 tsp. vanilla extract
- 25 Golden Oreos 2 Tbsp. unsalted butter, melted
- 1 1/2 containers (8 ounces each) Cool Whip Topping
- 1 pound fresh strawberries, hulled and sliced and patted dry

Directions
1. Whisk pudding, milk, and vanilla in a medium sized bowl. Let it sit while you prepare the crust.
2. Crush the cookies in a large gallon sized ziploc bag using a rolling pin. Reserve 1/2 cup of the cookie crumbs. Place the 2 Tbsp. melted butter in the bag and press with your hands to work the butter through the remaining cookie crumbs. Pour crumbs into a 9" square baking dish. The crust won't be solid, it'll stay crumbly.
3. Fold 8 oz. of the whipped topping into the pudding. Place half the pudding mixture on top of the crust. Place the strawberries in a single layer over the pudding. Spread remaining pudding mix over the top of the berries. Top with more whipped topping and sprinkle the remaining cookies over the top.
4. Chill for at least 4 hours before serving.

Lana's Favorite

Strawberry Shortcake

Ingredients
- 2/3 cup sugar
- 1/4 cup shortening
- 1 large egg
- 1 tsp. vanilla extract
- 1/4 tsp. salt
- 1-1/2 cups all-purpose flour
- 2 tsp. baking powder
- 1/2 cup milk

Many towns and villages in Alaska do not have road access to the outside. The capital, Juneau, does not, and neither does Nome. There are many more!

Directions
1. In a bowl, cream sugar and shortening. Add egg and vanilla; beat well. Combine dry ingredients and add alternately with milk to the creamed mixture.
2. Spread in a greased 9" square baking pan. Bake at 350° for 20-25 minutes. Cool on wire rack.
3. Garnish with berries and a dollop of whipped cream. Serve immediately. Yield: 9 servings.

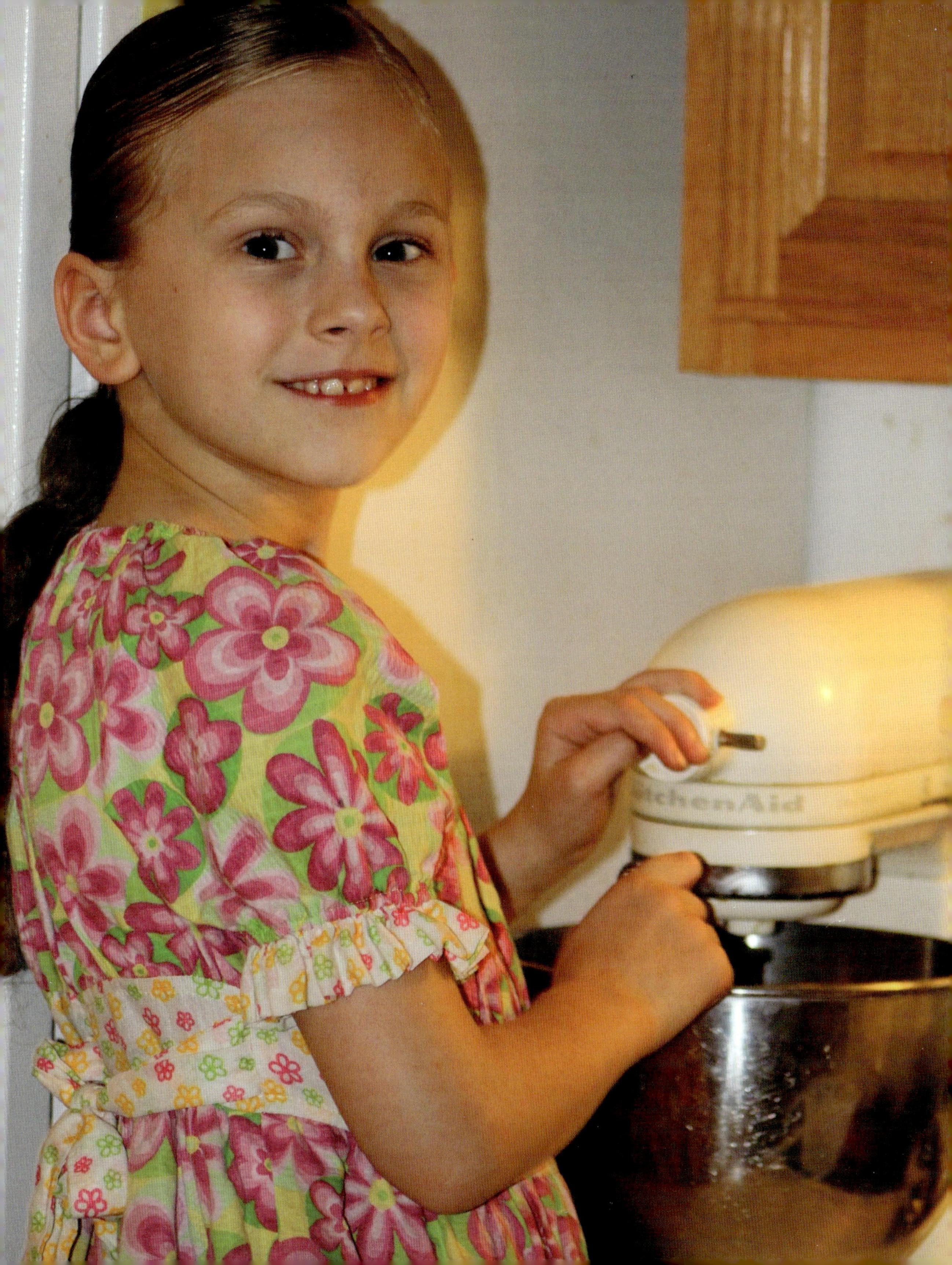
KitchenAid

Mint Chip Lush

Ingredients
- 20 Oreo cookies
- 2 Tbsp. unsalted butter, melted
- 8 oz. cream cheese
- 1/4 cup granulated sugar
- 1 tsp. vanilla extract
- 1/4-1/2 tsp. peppermint extract
- 1 (8 oz.) container whipped topping
- 1/2 cup mini chocolate chips
- 1 (approx. 3.4 ounce) box instant chocolate pudding mix
- 1 1/4 cups milk
- 5-7 drops green food coloring
- Additional mini chocolate chips or crushed cookies topping

Directions
1. Place cookies in a large resealable bag. Seal all but one inch of the bag and gently crush the cookies using a rolling pin. Pour melted butter into the bag and mix gently with your hands. Pour the crushed cookies into a 9"x9" baking dish. Spread evenly over the bottom. (The crust will not completely join together as a pie crust will.)
2. Beat cream cheese in a large bowl with a hand mixer until smooth. Mix in sugar, vanilla and 1/4 teaspoon peppermint extract. Add more peppermint extract, up to 1/2 teaspoon total, as desired for your personal taste. Fold in 1/2 the container (about 1 1/2 cups) whipped topping. Fold in chocolate chips. Add green food coloring and gently stir to fold in the color. Spread the mint layer over the cookie layer.
3. Mix the pudding mix with the milk. Whisk for 30 seconds. Let sit for a few minutes until the pudding thickens, then spread over mint layer.
4. Top with the remaining whipped topping and sprinkle with additional chocolate chips or crushed cookies. Cover and chill at least 2 hours before serving. Eat within 3 days.

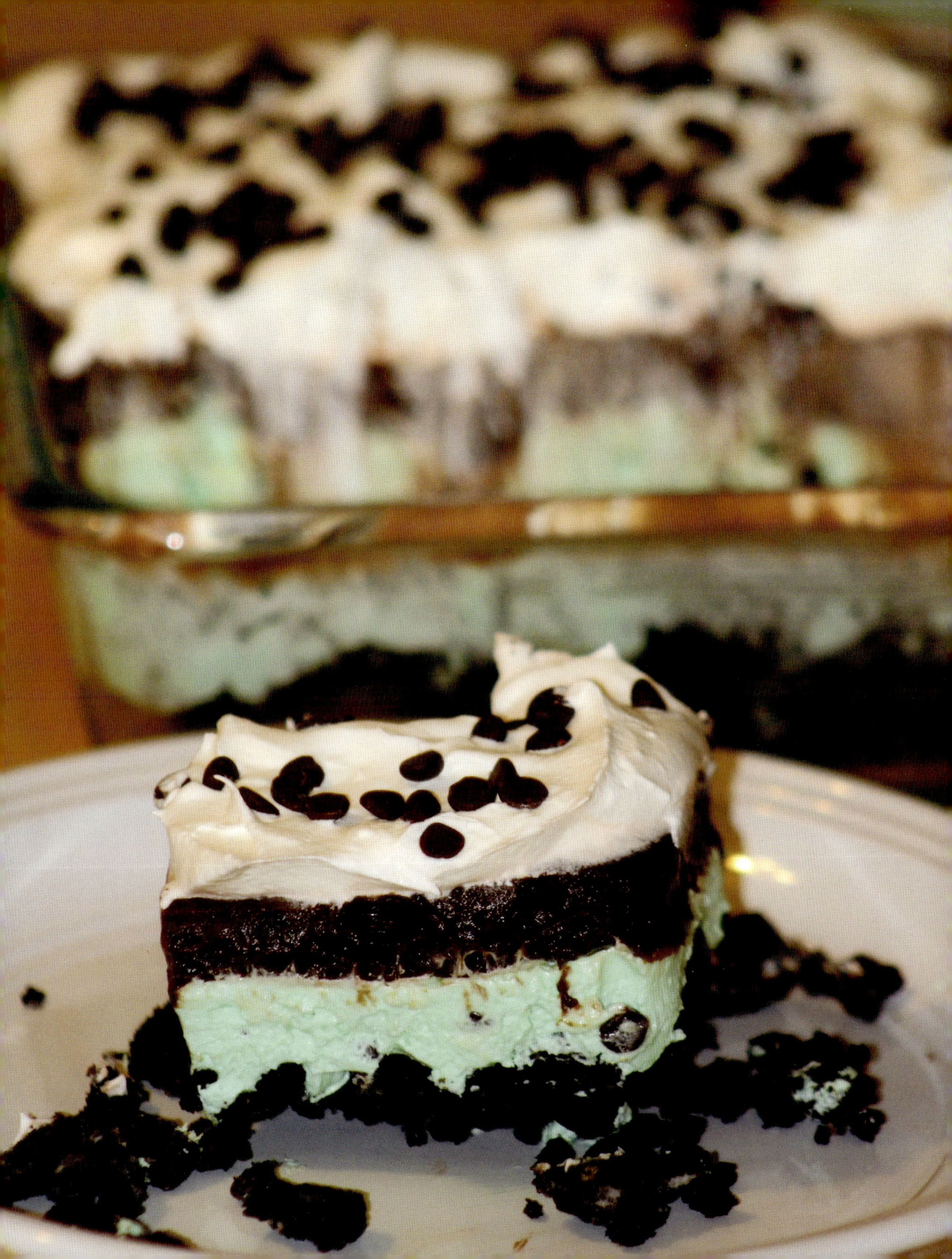

Fried Ice Cream Dessert

Ingredients

- 1/2 cup butter (1 stick)
- 1 cup sugar
- 1/2 tsp. salt
- 3 cups crushed cornflakes
- 1-1.75-quart container vanilla ice cream (real ice cream only)
- 1-8 oz. tub cool whip, thawed
- 3/4 tsp. cinnamon
- Honey for drizzling

Directions

1. Set ice cream out to soften up at room temperature for about 30 minutes.
2. Meanwhile, melt butter in a large skillet over medium-high heat then add sugar and salt. Stir and continue cooking until the sugar is thoroughly incorporated into the butter and the mixture starts to bubble (about 2-3 minutes). Add cornflakes and continue cooking, constantly stirring, for 5-6 minutes or until the cornflakes are slightly caramelized and browned. Be careful not to cook too long or the sugar will burn.
3. Add a little more than half of the cornflakes to the bottom of a 13x9 baking dish (more than 1/2 but not quite 2/3). Using your hand, pat the cornflakes into a level crust in the bottom of the dish. Let crust cool to room temperature.
4. In a stand mixer using the paddle attachment or large bowl using big ole spoon, mix ice cream, cool whip and cinnamon just until thoroughly combined.
5. Spread ice cream mixture evenly over cornflake layer. Sprinkle top of ice cream evenly with remaining cornflakes. Cover and return to freezer. Freeze "cake" for 4 hours before serving.
6. Drizzle each portion with honey before serving.

Pina Colada Fluff

Ingredients
- 1 3.4 oz. vanilla instant pudding mix
- 1 20 oz. can crushed pineapple (do not drain!)
- 1 8 oz. container Cool Whip - thawed
- 1 tsp. rum extract
- 2 cup miniature marshmallows
- 1 cup shredded sweetened coconut
- 1/2 cup chopped nuts (your favorite)

Alaska has no vehicle inspections, although police can pull over cars if they are falling apart.

Instructions
1. Combine pudding mix and the entire can of crushed pineapple in a large bowl.
2. Stir until completely combined.
3. Fold in Cool Whip, rum extract, marshmallows, coconut, and nuts,
4. Chill until ready to served.

Mocha Mud Pie Dessert

Ingredients
- 1/4 cup water
- 2 tsp. instant coffee (or one single-serve packet)
- 20 Oreos
- 2 Tbsp. unsalted butter, softened
- 8 oz. cream cheese, softened
- 1/4 cup powdered sugar
- 1 (8 oz.) container Cool Whip, divided
- 1 box (3.9 oz.) instant chocolate or chocolate fudge pudding mix
- 1 cup milk
- 1/3 cup sliced almonds
- 2 Tbsp. hot fudge ice cream topping, warmed

Directions
1. Mix the water and the instant coffee in a measuring cup and let it sit for a few minutes to dissolve.
2. Meanwhile, make the crust. Place the Oreos in a a gallon size ziploc bag and seal it almost all the way. (Roll with a rolling pin until you get coarse crumbs. Place crumbs in a medium sized bowl and stir in softened butter.
3. Press the crust into a 9"x9" baking dish. The crust won't be solid, it will be more chunky and loose.
4. Place cream cheese in a large mixing bowl. Mix with a hand mixer until smooth. Whisk in powdered sugar and coffee.
5. Stir in one cup of cool whip. Gently spread over the crust.
6. Add the pudding mix and milk and whisk until smooth. Once pudding has set up (just a minute or so), spread over cream cheese layer.
7. Spread the remaining Cool Whip over the top.
8. Cover and chill for 4 hours or overnight.
9. Before serving, place warmed hot fudge ice cream topping in a sandwich sized ziploc bag. Cut off one tip and pipe criss-cross stripes on top of the Cool Whip. Sprinkle with almonds.

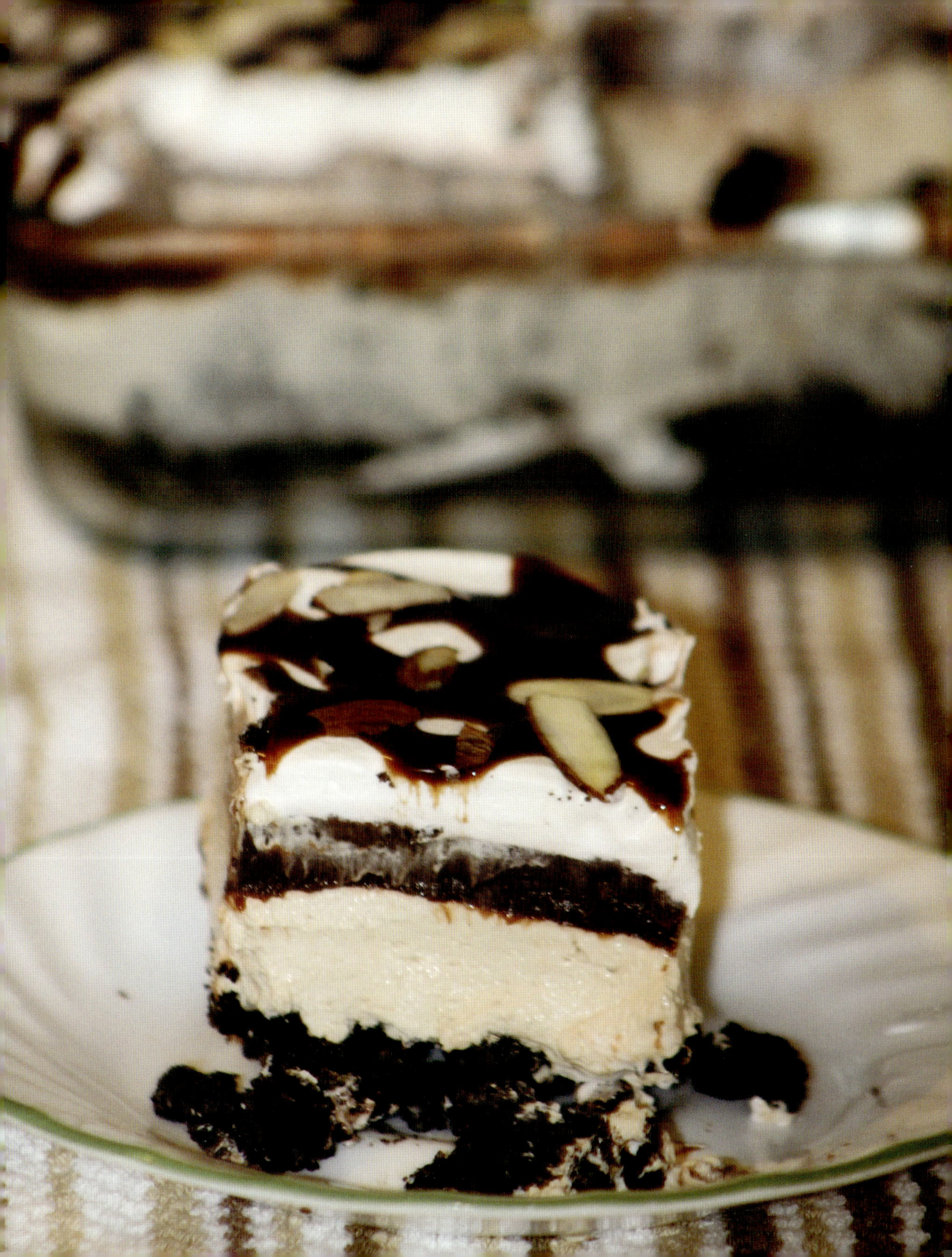

Toasted Coconut Pudding

Ingredients
- 1/2 cup melted margarine
- 1 cup chopped pecans
- 1/4 cup brown sugar
- 1 cup flour
- 1 1/2 cups coconut
- prepared vanilla pudding
- whipped topping

Directions
1. Mix first five ingredients together and spread on a pan.
2. Bake at 325º for about 30 minutes, or until lightly browned, stirring occasionally.
3. Mix prepared vanilla pudding and whipped topped together gently.
4. Layer with cooled pecan mixture in a serving dish, and serve immediately.

Pistachio Ice Cream Desert

Ingredients
- 1 cup crushed butter-flavored crackers
- 1/4 cup butter, melted
- 3/4 cup cold milk
- 1 package (3.4 ounces) instant pistachio pudding mix
- 1 quart vanilla ice cream, softened
- 1 carton (8 oz.) frozen whipped topping, thawed
- 2 packages (1.4 oz. each) Heath candy bars, crushed

Directions
1. In a small bowl, combine cracker crumbs and butter. Press into an ungreased 9-in. square baking pan. Bake at 325° for 7-10 minutes or until lightly browned. Cool on a wire rack.
2. Meanwhile, in a large bowl, whisk milk and pudding mix for 2 minutes (mixture will be thick). Stir in ice cream; pour over crust. Cover and freeze for 2 hours or until firm.
3. Spread with whipped topping; sprinkle with crushed candy bars. Cover and freeze for 1 hour or until firm. Yield: 9 servings.

Vanilla Bean Cheesecake

Ingredients

Graham Cracker Crust
- 1 1/2 cup finely crushed graham crackers
- 1/4 cup light brown sugar
- 1 stick unsalted butter, melted
- 1/2 tsp. vanilla extract

Cheesecake Filling
- 16 oz. cream cheese, softened
- 2 sticks unsalted butter, softened
- 1 cup granulated sugar
- 1 cup sour cream
- 2 Tbsp. corn starch
- 1 vanilla bean pod, beans extracted or 1 Tbsp. vanilla bean paste

White Chocolate Mousse
- 4 oz. white chocolate baking squares
- 1 cup heavy whipping cream
- 4 Tbsp. powdered sugar
- 4 oz. cream cheese, softened

Directions

Graham Cracker Crust
1. Preheat oven to 375° and line a spring-form pan with parchment paper.
2. In a medium bowl, combine crushed graham crackers and brown sugar and mix with a fork
3. Add the melted butter and vanilla extract and mix until fully incorporated
4. Press into the bottom of the lined spring-form pan and bake for 8-10 minutes
5. Remove from oven and let cool

Cheesecake Filling
1. Preheat oven to 320°
2. In a stand mixer, beat the cream cheese, butter and sugar until light and fluffy
3. Add the sour cream, corn starch and vanilla beans and mix until the mixture is smooth and creamy
4. Pour over the graham cracker crust and bake for one hour. The filling will be jiggly in the center when you remove from oven
5. Remove from the oven and place on a heat safe surface for one hour. Do not remove the spring-form pan. You will remove it right before serving!
6. Place into the refrigerator overnight to set, or at least 6 hours

White Chocolate Mousse
1. Place mixing bowl in freezer or refrigerator to chill.
2. Melt white chocolate squares and let cool.
3. In the cold mixing bowl, beat the heavy cream until it forms soft peaks, gradually add powdered sugar and continue whipping until it forms stiff peaks.
4. Place in refrigerator to keep chilled.
5. In another bowl, beat the melted white chocolate and cream cheese together with a spatula until light and fluffy.
6. Take the whipped cream and stir it into the white chocolate and cream cheese mixture.
7. Place back into the refrigerator to chill overnight. Keep refrigerated until you are ready to put the mousse onto the cheesecake.
8. Once you are ready to serve, spread the mousse over the top of the cheesecake and then remove the spring-form pan and the parchment paper.
Top with whipped cream, berries, chocolate or all three!

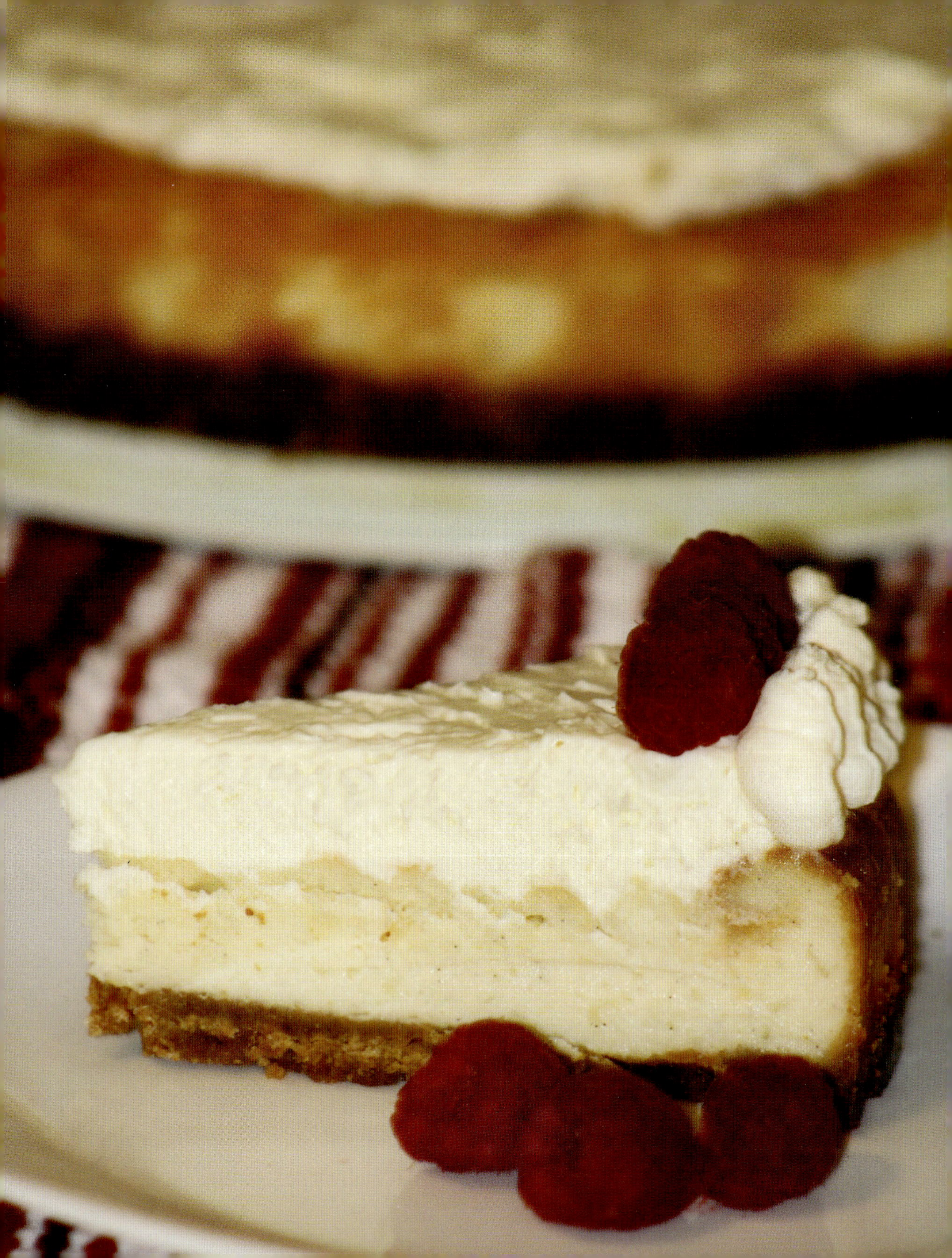

Rainbow Jello

Ingredients
- 6 (3 ounce) packages Jello gelatin (blue raspberry, grape, lime, orange, lemon, strawberry)
- 2 cups sour cream

Directions
1. Mix each package of Jello, separately, with 1 cup boiling water.
2. Divide in half. Pour first half in pan.
3. Chill in refrigerator for 10 to 15 minutes.
4. Mix second half with 1/3 cup sour cream or Cool Whip.
5. Pour over first layer; chill. Continue layers alternately until all 12 layers are done.
6. layer red, orange, yellow, green, blue, purple

Samantha's Favorite

Reese's Peanut Butter Truffles

Ingredients

- 16 oz. Nutter Butter Cookies
- 8 oz. cream cheese
- 8 oz. Reese's Mini Peanut Butter Cups, each one quartered
- 12 oz. milk chocolate chips
- 3/4 Tbsp. shortening
- 1 Tbsp. sprinkles (optional)

Directions

1. Blend the Nutter Butter cookies in a food processor until they are fine crumbs. Break up the cream cheese into chunks and blend that together with the crumbs in the food processor until well blended.
2. Remove blade or transfer dough to another bowl. Gently fold in the quartered Reese's peanut butter cups. I used the very small mini Reese's that come unwrapped.
3. Roll into 1 inch balls and place on a cookie sheet lined with waxed paper or parchment paper. Stick in the freezer for about 30 to 40 minutes.
4. Melt the chocolate chips and shortening in a microwave safe bowl stirring every 30 seconds until smooth.
5. Dip the frozen balls into the melted chocolate. Cover them completely with chocolate, then lift up and gently tap to remove the excess chocolate.
6. Set back onto the cookie sheet covered in waxed paper. Immediately add the sprinkles before the chocolate sets up.
7. The chocolate will set up quickly because the balls are so cold from being in the freezer. Makes about 30 to 35 truffles.

Pumpkin Roll Cake

Ingredients
- 6 Tbsp. butter, softened
- 1 1/2 cups granulated sugar
- 2 large eggs
- 1 (15 oz.) can pumpkin puree
- 1/4 cup milk
- 1 tsp. vanilla
- 2 cups all-purpose flour
- 1 tsp. ground cinnamon
- 2 tsp. pumpkin pie spice
- 1 tsp. baking soda
- 1/2 tsp. baking powder
- 1/4 tsp. salt

Cream Cheese Filling
- 8 ounces cream cheese, softened
- 1/4 cup granulated sugar
- 1 large egg
- 1 teaspoon vanilla

Directions
1. Preheat oven to 350°. Spray a 9"x13" inch glass baking pan with non-stick spray. Set aside.
2. In a large bowl, cream butter and sugar together until fluffy. Add eggs, pumpkin, milk and vanilla. Mix to combine.
3. In a separate medium bowl, combine flour, cinnamon, pumpkin pie spice, baking powder, baking soda and salt. Gradually add dry ingredients to pumpkin mixture and stir until combined. Pour 2/3 of the pumpkin batter into prepared baking dish.

For Cream Cheese Filling
1. In a medium bowl, using an electric mixer, beat cream cheese until smooth. Add the egg, 1/4 cup sugar and teaspoon vanilla. Continue to beat until smooth and combined.
2. Spread cream cheese filling evenly over pumpkin batter in pan. Spoon the remaining pumpkin batter over cream cheese layer and smooth out in an even layer. Using a knife, trace the pan in a swirl motion to marble the cream cheese and pumpkin layers together.
3. Bake 30 to 35 minutes or until toothpick inserted in center comes out clean. Cool cake before slicing. Serve each slice with a dollop of whip cream, if desired. Enjoy!

Other books by

ALASKA ADVENTURE BOOKS

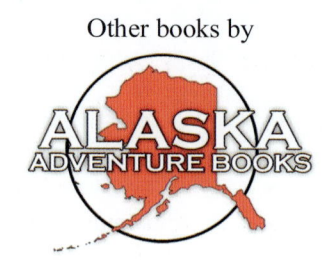

The *Adventures of a Traveling Dog Salesman* Series, by Matt Snader:

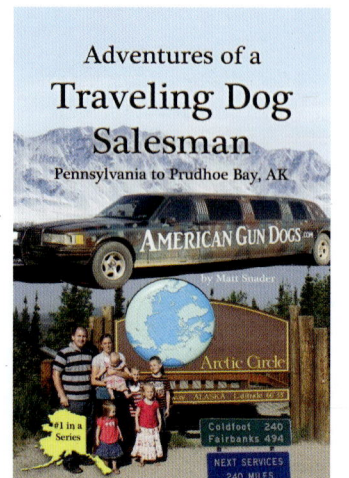

Book 1: Pennsylvania to Prudhoe Bay

In 2013 our family drove to Alaska from Pennsylvania in our camouflage limo. The rest is history! Starting out with a print run of 100, it sold out almost overnight. A second print run of 3,000 was ordered, which also sold out quickly. Now we are working through the third print run of 10,000.

Released in 2014. 80 Pages, full color. Suggested retail $9.99. Available at book stores and online at www.AlaskaAdventureBooks.com

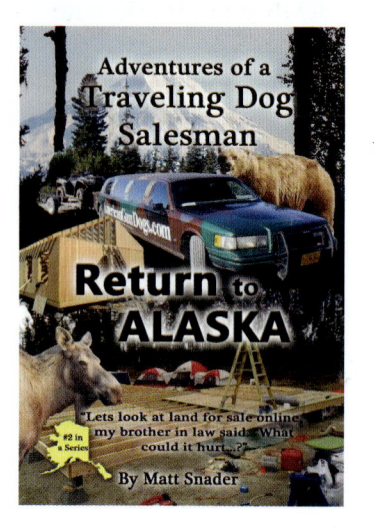

Book 2: Return to Alaska

While browsing real estate online in late 2014, we discovered 40 acres for $15,500. Not able to resist the lure of the North, we bought the land, and moved to Alaska, into the wilderness and "off the grid". This brought about some challenging and sometimes humorous situations. An earthquake, wildfire, cabin break in, and brown bear attack are included.

Released in 2015. 176 Pages, full color. Suggested retail $12.99. Available at book stores and online at www.AlaskaAdventureBooks.com

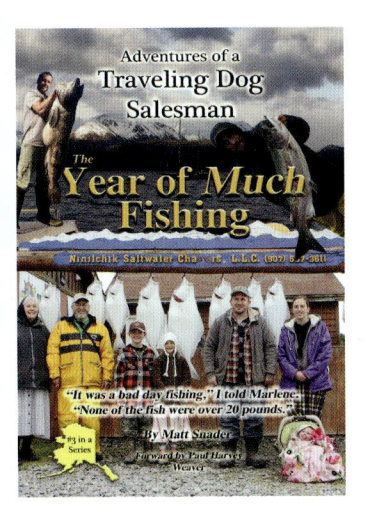

Book 3: The Year of Much Fishing

Visit Alaska again with the Snader family! This time, it's about fishing. From the mighty King Salmon to 50 pound Halibut, fishing in Alaska is rarely boring. Of course they do more than just fish-the wheel comes off the limo on a busy interstate highway. And could anything go wrong with buying a 27' boat off of Ebay and hauling it 4,000 miles to Alaska? How did 1,000 chickens end up in the cabin? And how did the Snader family end up crashing an invitation only, federal government Christmas tree party-with their church bishop, of all people?

Released in 2016. 224 Pages, full color. Suggested retail $13.99. Available at book stores and online at www.AlaskaAdventureBooks.com

Book 5: There is No Place Like Nome

Travel to Nome, Alaska, with the Snader Family! Learn all about Nome, Alaska, and of course experiencing it with the Snaders is never boring. From crashing a drone, to accidently taking live ammunition in the airplane carry on, it's rather eventful! Bonus: Get Josh's (Matt's brother) take on a trip with Matt and his family in an old motorhome purchased for $2,500 on a 4,000 mile road trip. Available in local book stores and online at www.AlaskaAdventureBooks.com

Releasing late 2016

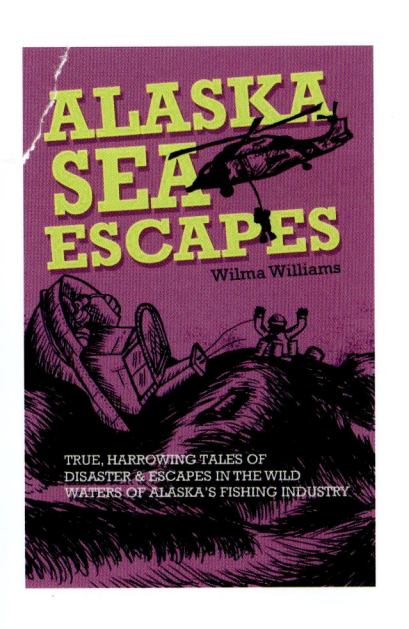

Alaska Sea Escapes

Read about 15 heart stopping situations off the coast of Alaska! Many of the ships sank in these accounts, which are all true. Matt's neighbor, Richard, was on the fated crab ship the *El Dan*. Sure to keep you on the edge of your seat!

Written by Homer, Alaska, resident Wilma Williams.

Originally published in 1998, and Rereleased in 2016. 128 Pages, B&W. Suggested retail $9.99. Available at book stores and online at www.AlaskaAdventureBooks.com

Notes: